The
GOOD APP
BOOK
OF
REPRODUCIBLE
PATTERNS
A
COLOSSAL
Collection
of
Captivating Images

BY NANCEE MCCLURE

Copyright © Good Apple, 1991

ISBN No. 0-86653-622-1

Printing No. 987654321

Good Apple
1204 Buchanan St., Box 299
Carthage, IL 62321-0299

SIMON & SCHUSTER *A Paramount Communications Company*

IT'S FINALLY HERE!

GOOD APPLE delivers the "goods" once again! Created just for you, the busy teacher, **The Good Apple Book of Reproducible Patterns** is packed with over 600 versatile patterns that you will use over and over again in a variety of ways. Here are just a few.

✖ **Create and Revitalize Learning Centers.** Right at your fingertips you'll have hundreds of easily adaptable images to help you get your messages across. Take a look below for just a few ways these patterns can be used.

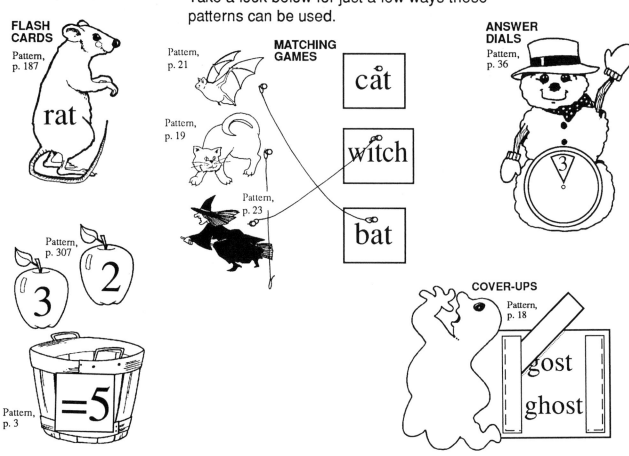

FLASH CARDS
Pattern, p. 187

rat

Pattern, p. 21

MATCHING GAMES

Pattern, p. 19

Pattern, p. 23

cat

witch

bat

ANSWER DIALS
Pattern, p. 36

Pattern, p. 307

3   2

Pattern, p. 3

=5

COVER-UPS
Pattern, p. 18

gost

ghost

✖ **Custom-design Awards** to boost self-esteem and build motivation! Included on page 128 are several faces that you can use to add personality to any of the inanimate images in this pattern book.

Patterns, pp. 341, 342

You're a Blue Ribbon Reader!

SUPER SPELLER

MATH MASTER!

#1 READER!

GA1341

✖ **Banish the "Bulletin Board Blues"** with these captivating images and helpful suggestions on how to use them. Creating active bulletin boards will stimulate your students' curiosity and provide them with a "hands-on" learning experience. There are plenty of holiday and seasonal images so your classroom will be a festive place any time of the year!

✖ **Make Room Decorations Manageable in No Time** at all with these ready-to-use patterns.

Pattern, p. 41

Pattern, p. 46

Pattern, p. 29

Pattern, pp. 103,104

These patterns are designed to stimulate a teacher's imagination. With your teaching objectives and your students' grade level in mind, these images can be adapted and transformed into exciting, creative teaching tools. Assembling learning centers and bulletin boards that "talk back" requires a little practice. A wonderful tool that teaches the mechanical aspects of assembly is **Teaching Is Off the Wall** published by Fearon Teacher Aids. With a little time and energy, the captivating images in this colossal book will become dynamic teaching tools that interact with your students.

This generous book of appealing images will soon become an invaluable resource in your classroom. These patterns can also be used for:

Greeting Card Art	Poster Art	Story Starters
Arts and Crafts Activities	Signs	Mobiles
Party Decorations	Games	Flash Cards
Centerpieces	Gameboards	Calendars

GA1341

TABLE OF CONTENTS

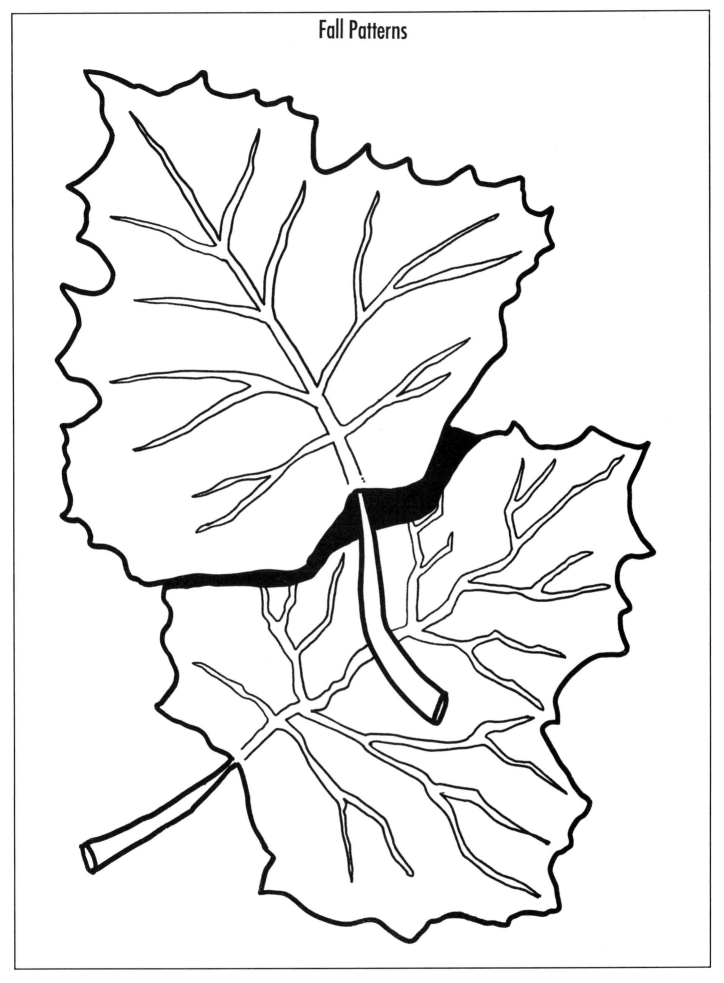

GA1341

GA1341

GA1341

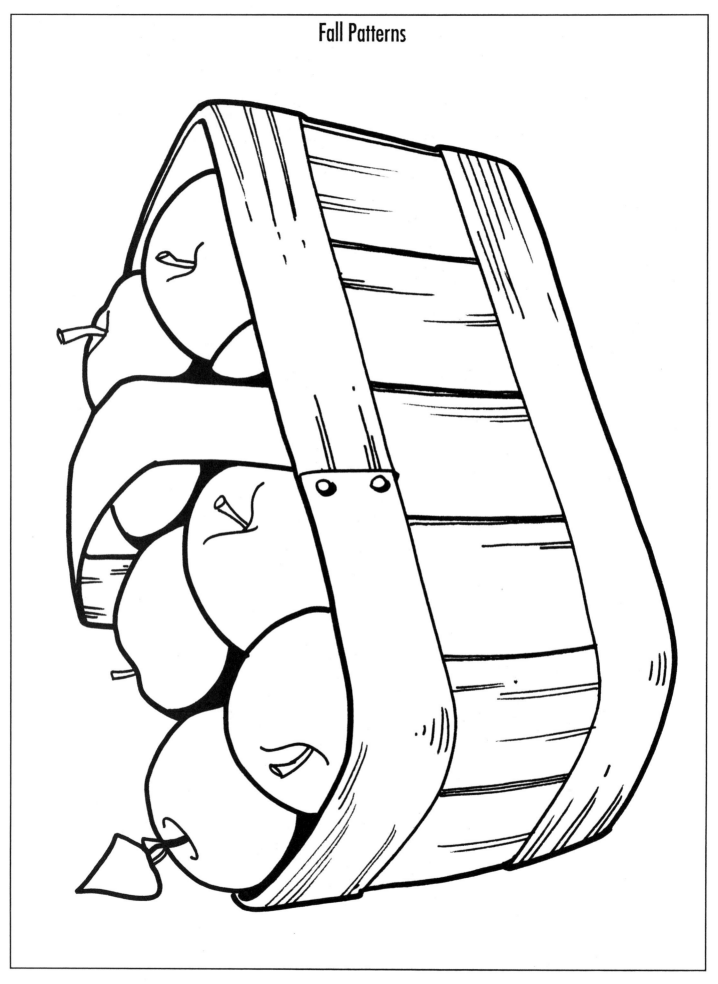

GA1341

Fall Patterns

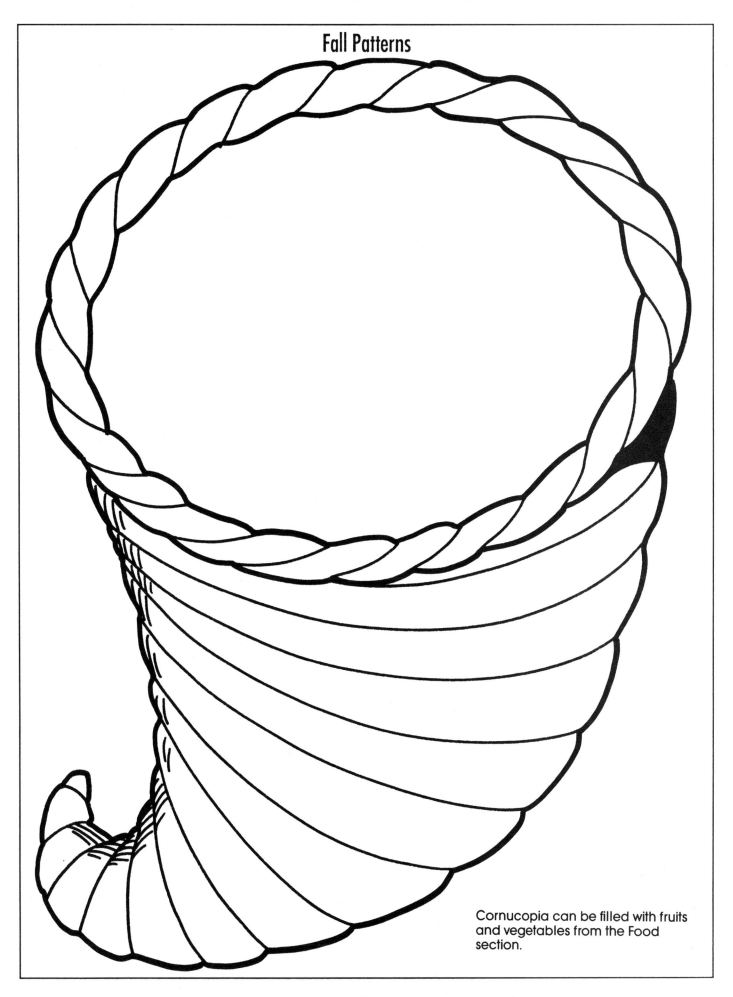

Cornucopia can be filled with fruits and vegetables from the Food section.

5

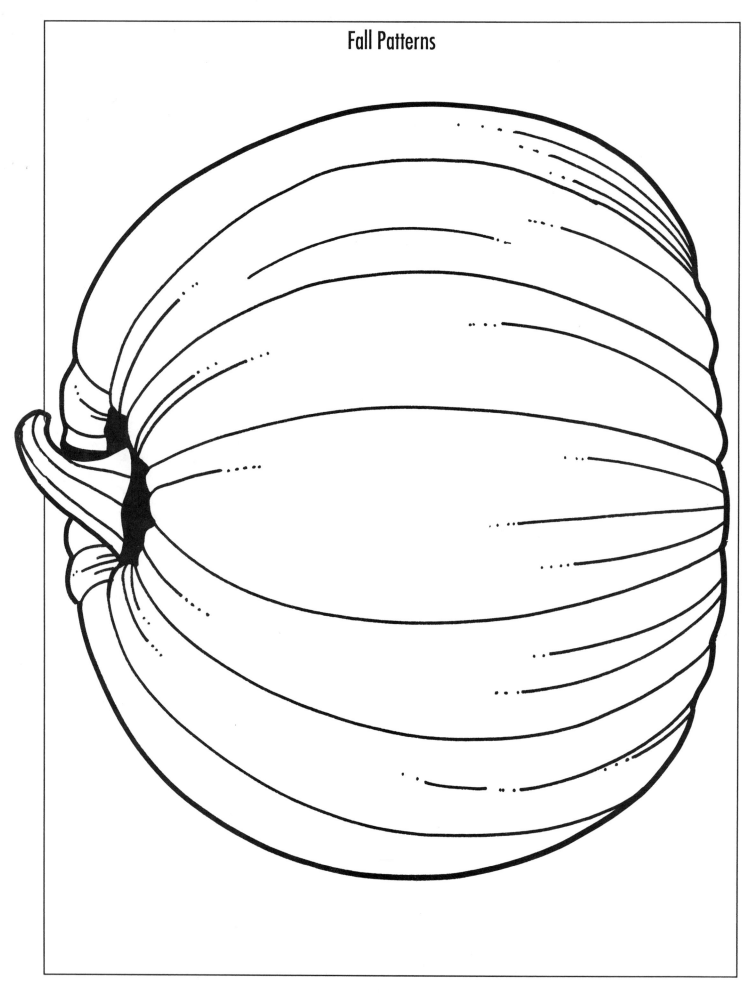

GA1341

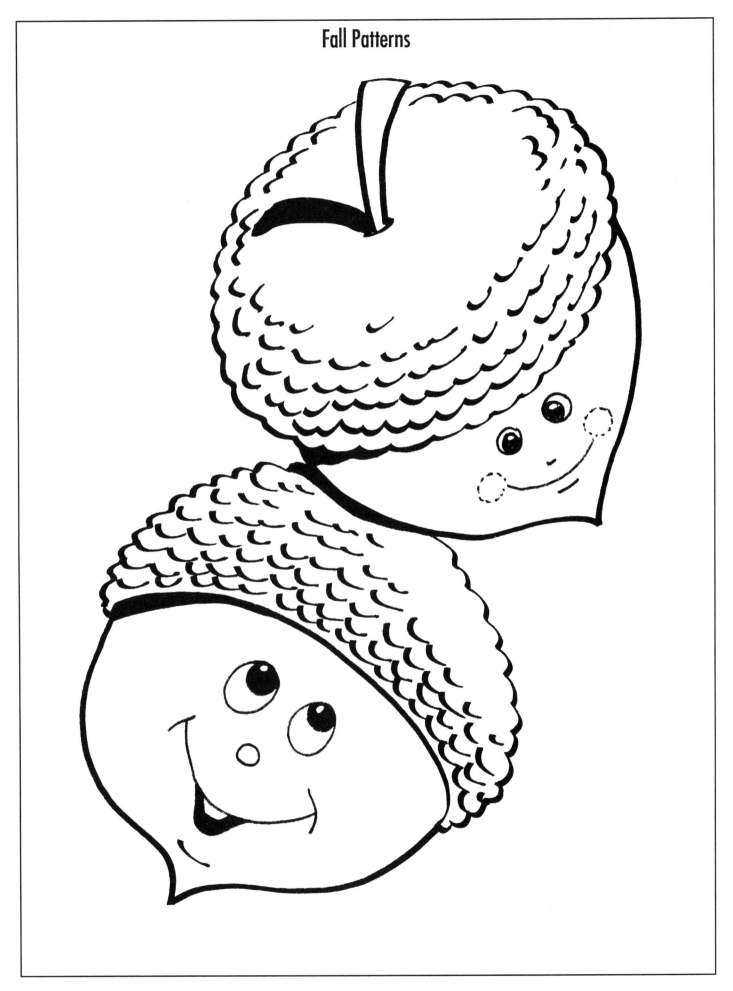

GA1341

Fall Patterns

8

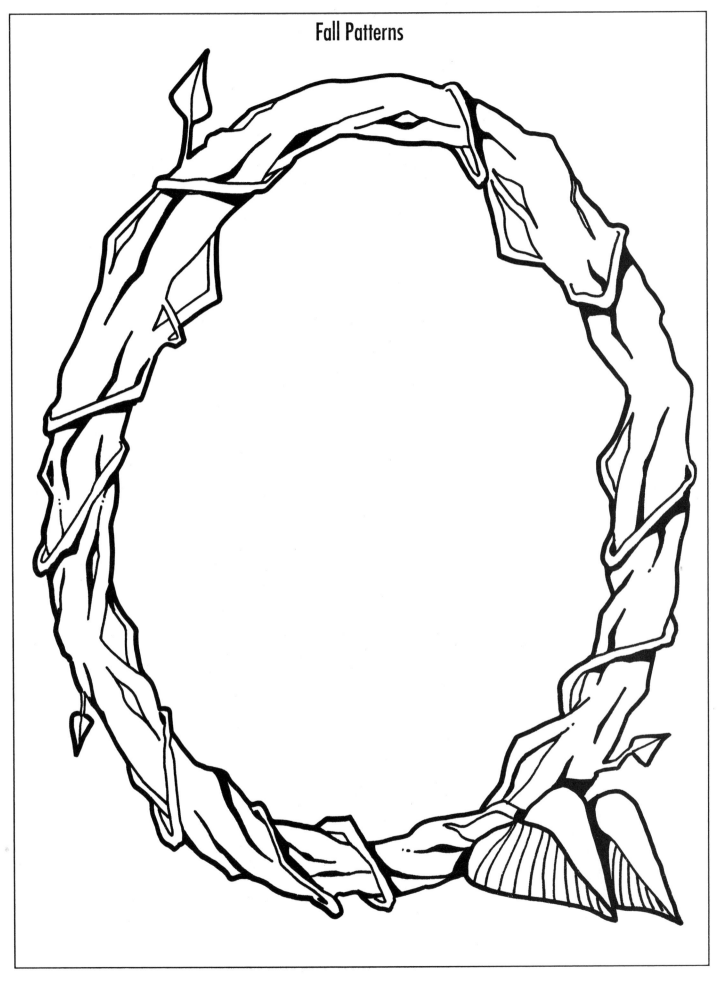

GA1341

10

11

GA1341

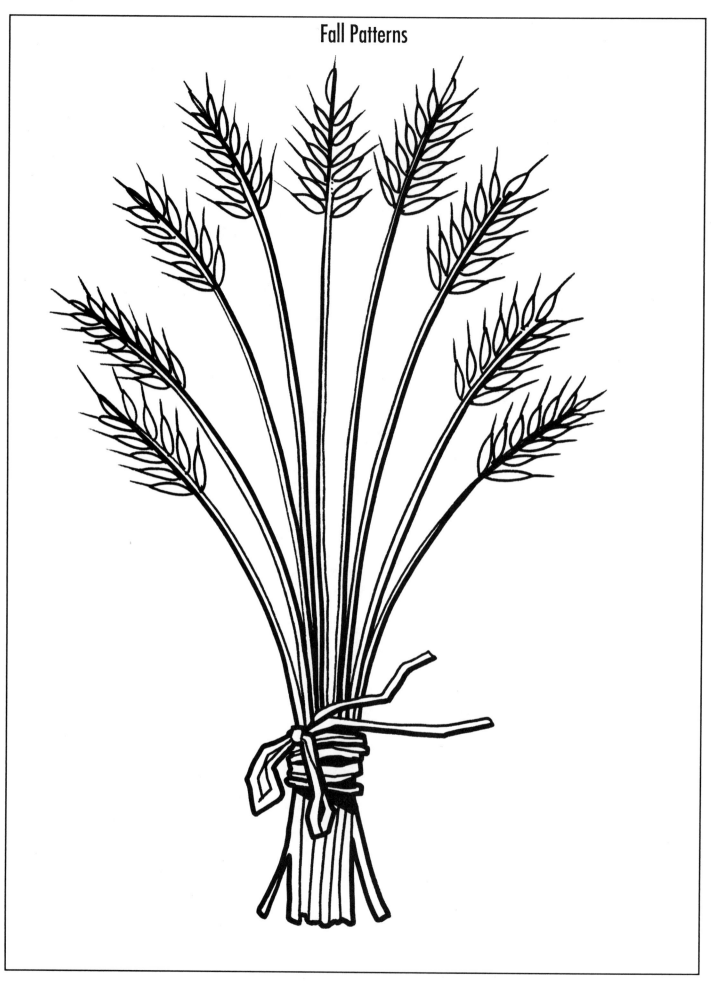

Columbus Day

GA1341

GA1341

GA1341

GA1341

GA1341

Halloween

18

GA1341

GA1341

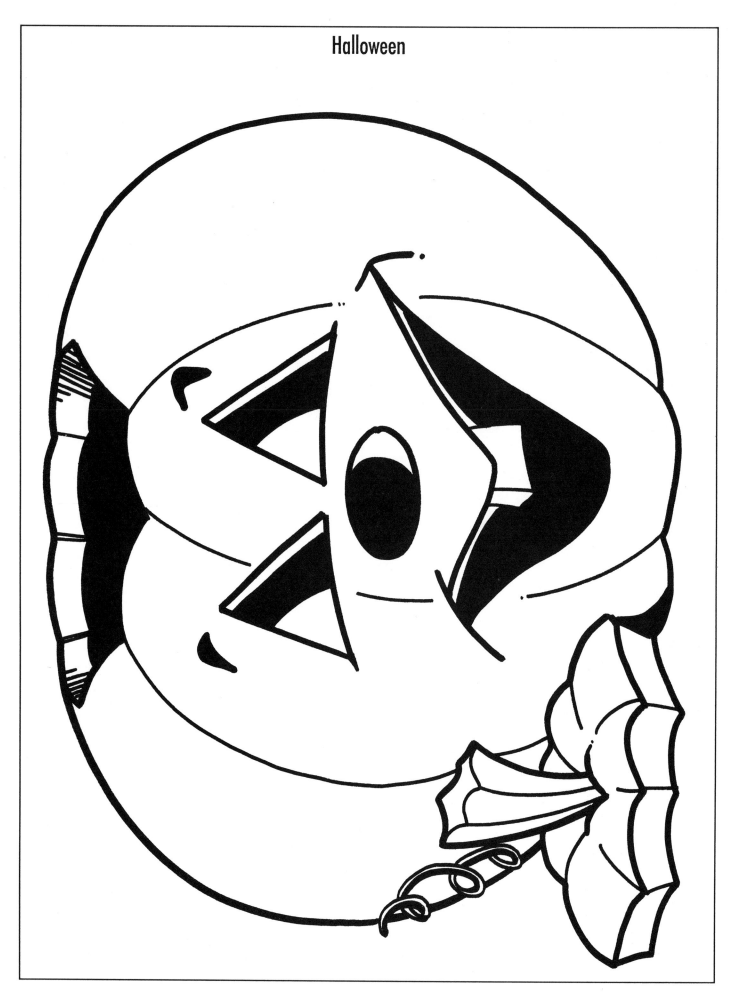

20

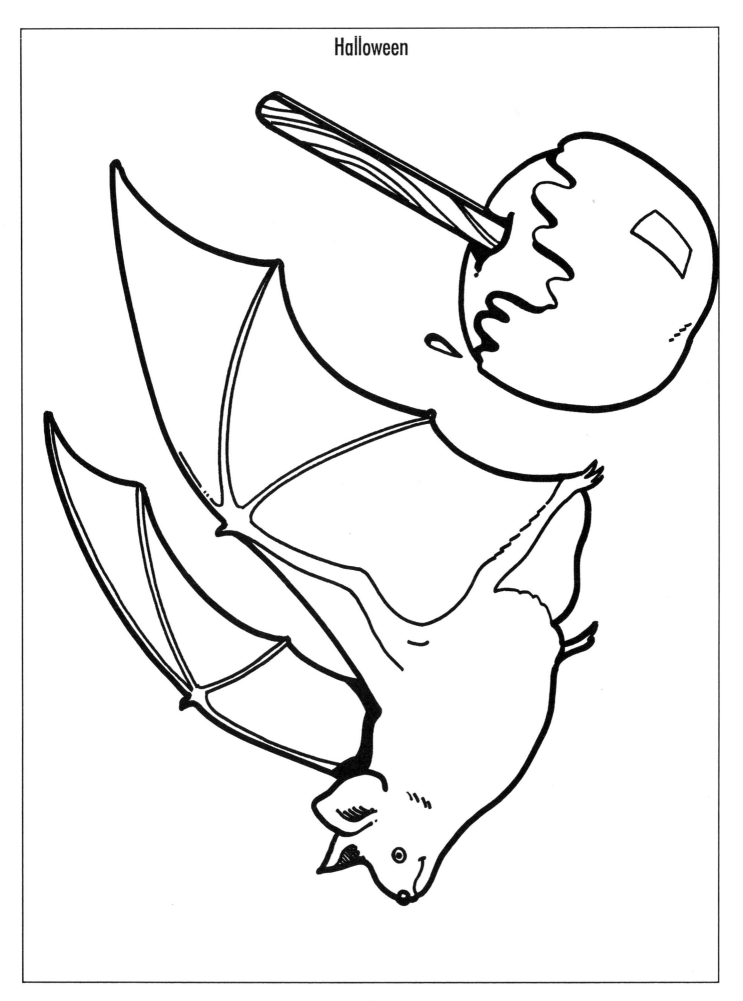

GA1341

TRICK OR TREAT!

22

GA1341

Halloween

23

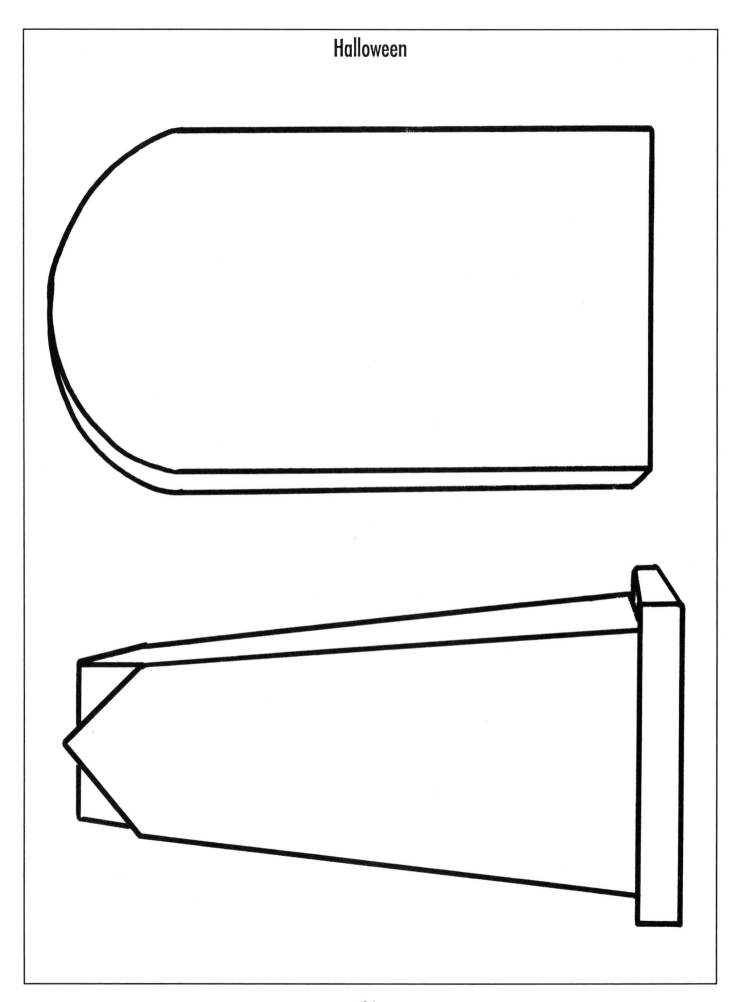

25

GA1341

GA1341

GA1341

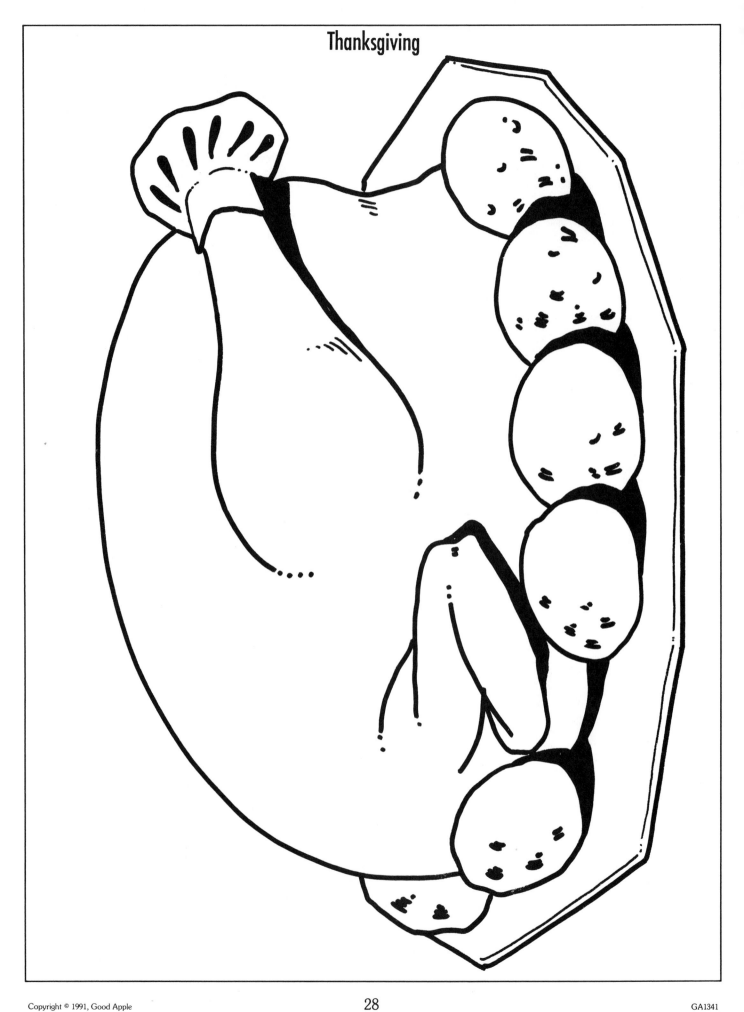

28

GA1341

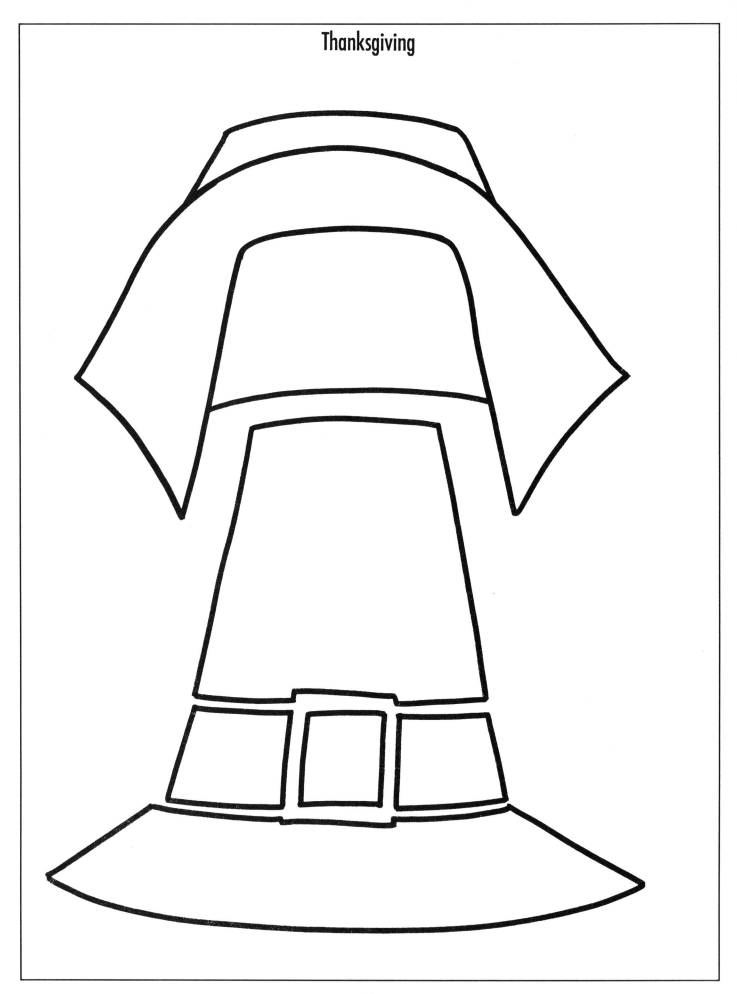

30

GA1341

GA1341

Thanksgiving

Thanksgiving

33

Thanksgiving

34

GA1341

36

GA1341

Winter Patterns

GA1341

Winter Patterns

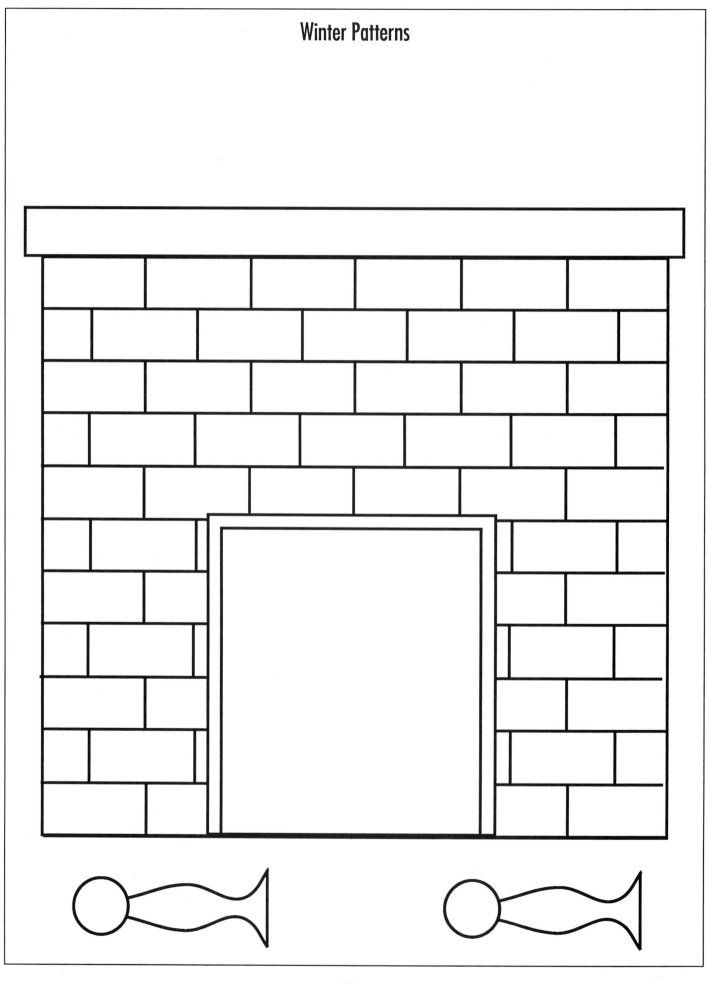

GA1341

40

GA1341

GA1341

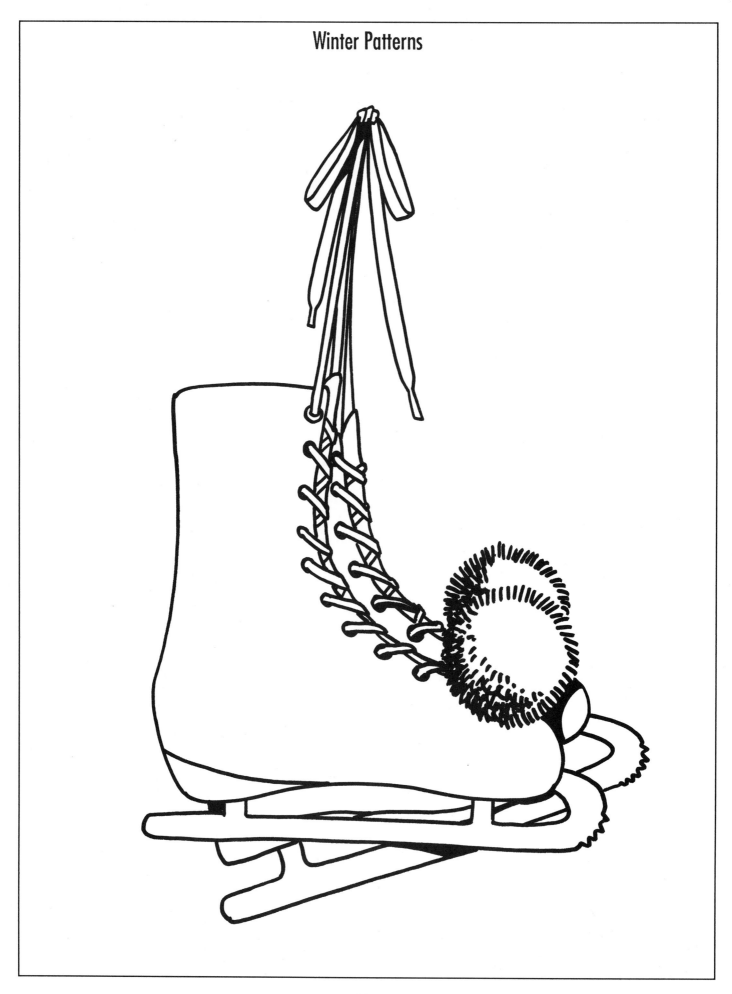

42

GA1341

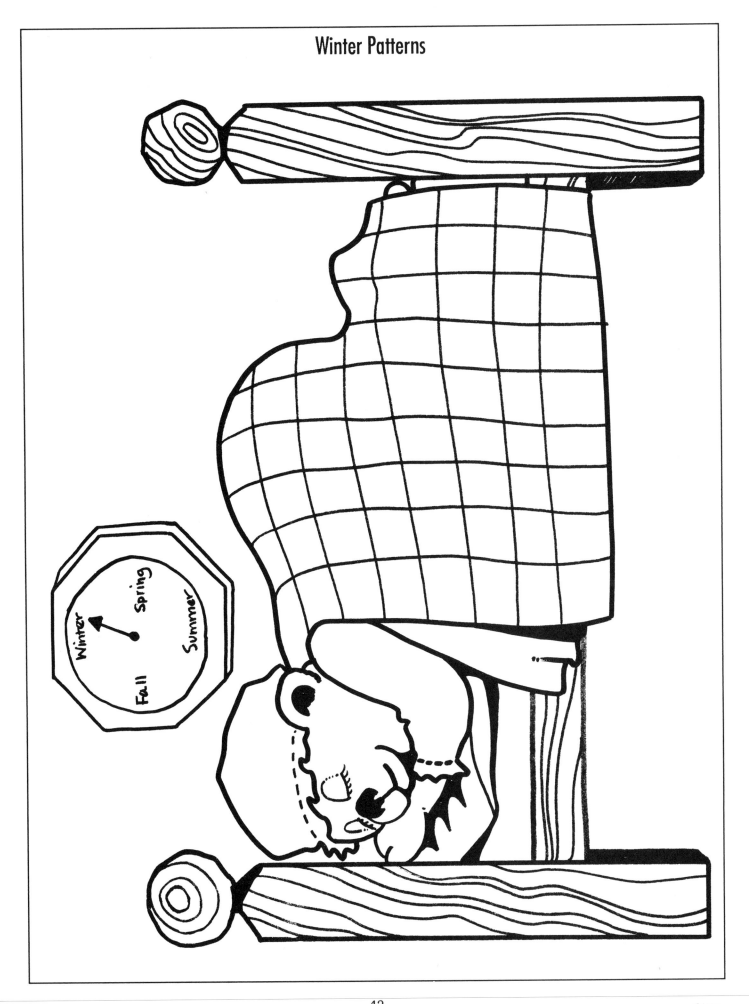

GA1341

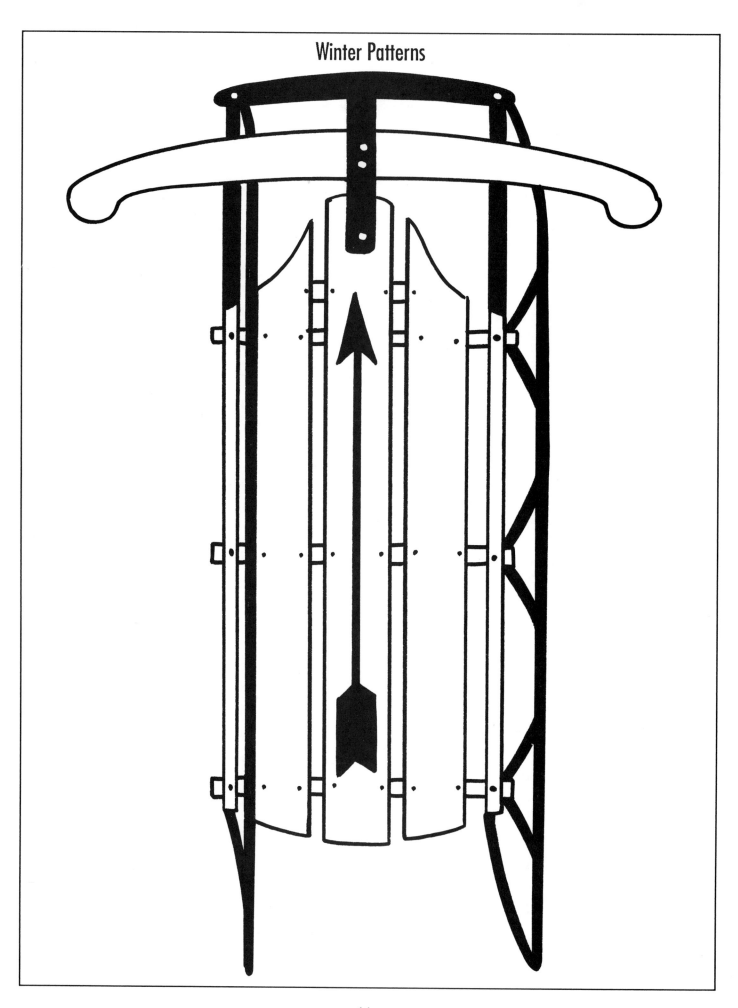

44

GA1341

46

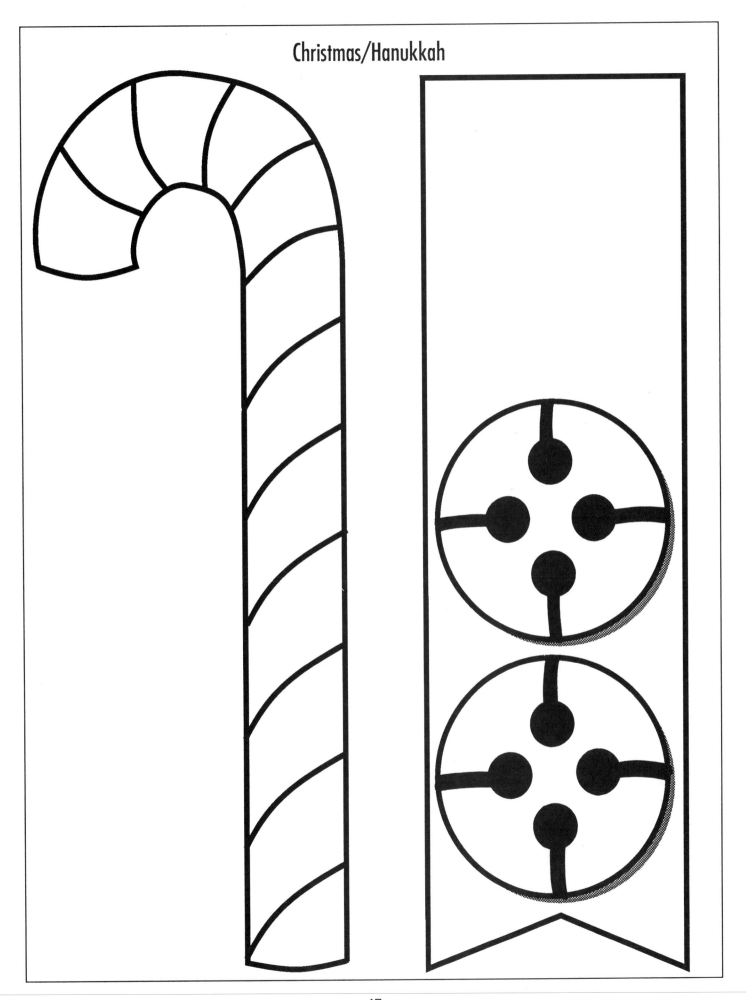

GA1341

Christmas/Hanukkah

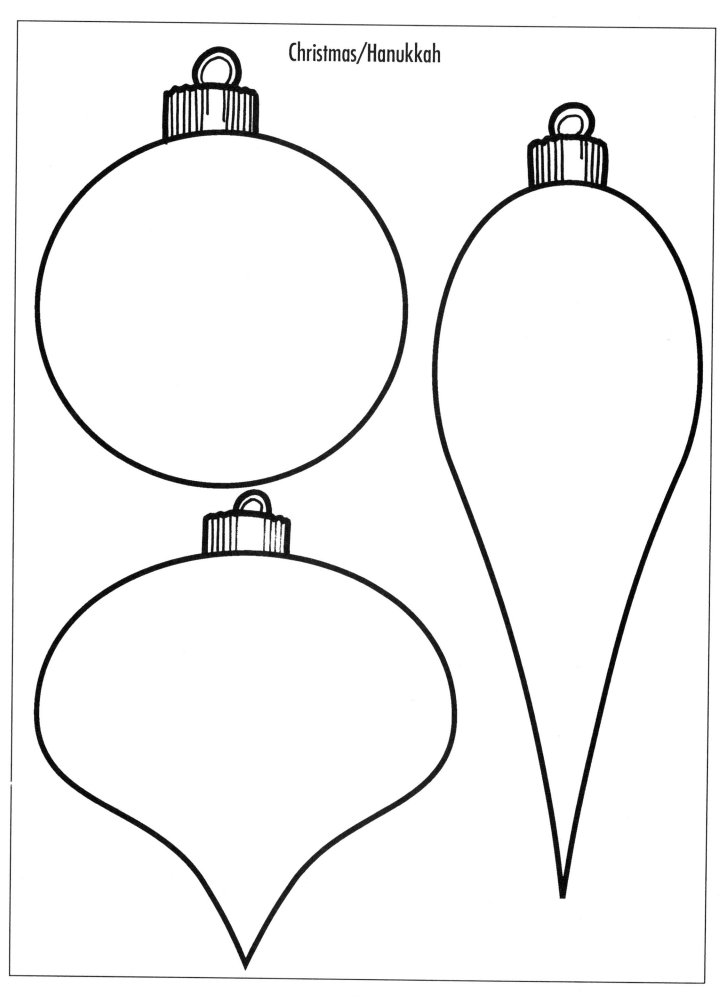

48

GA1341

GA1341

Christmas/Hanukkah

51

GA1341

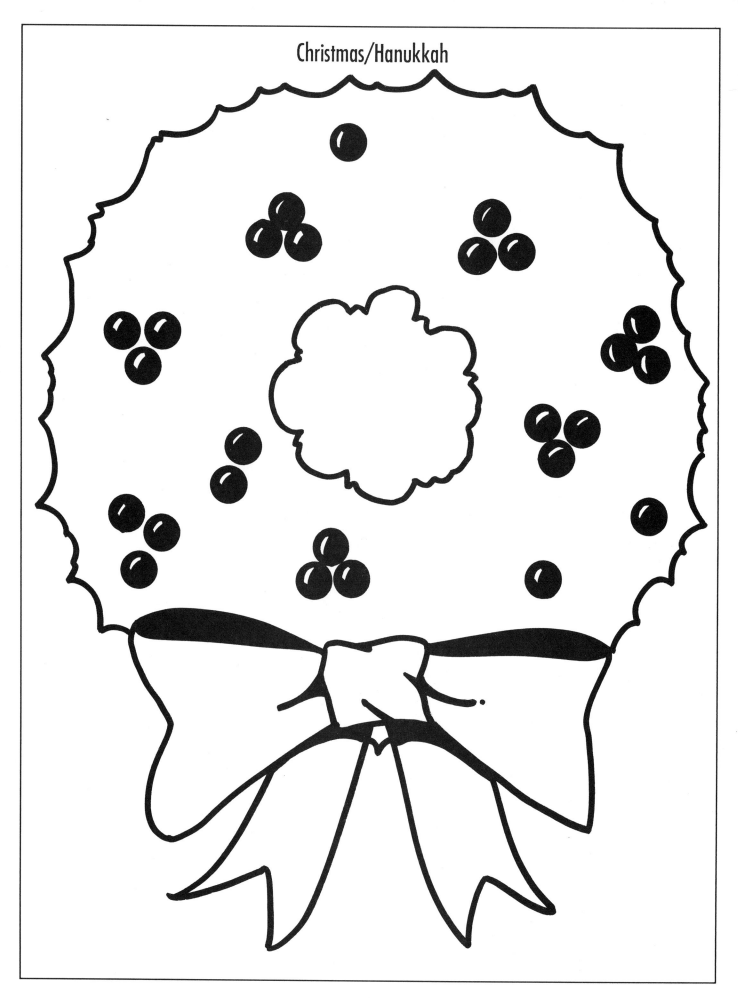

GA1341

GA1341

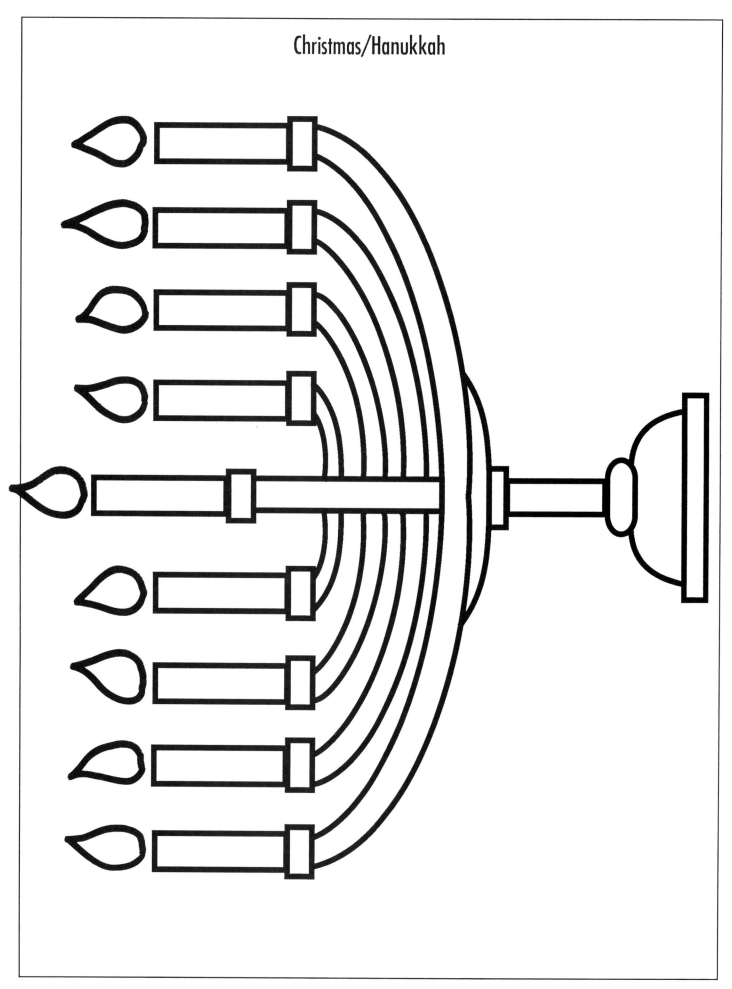

GA1341

GA1341

Christmas/Hanukkah

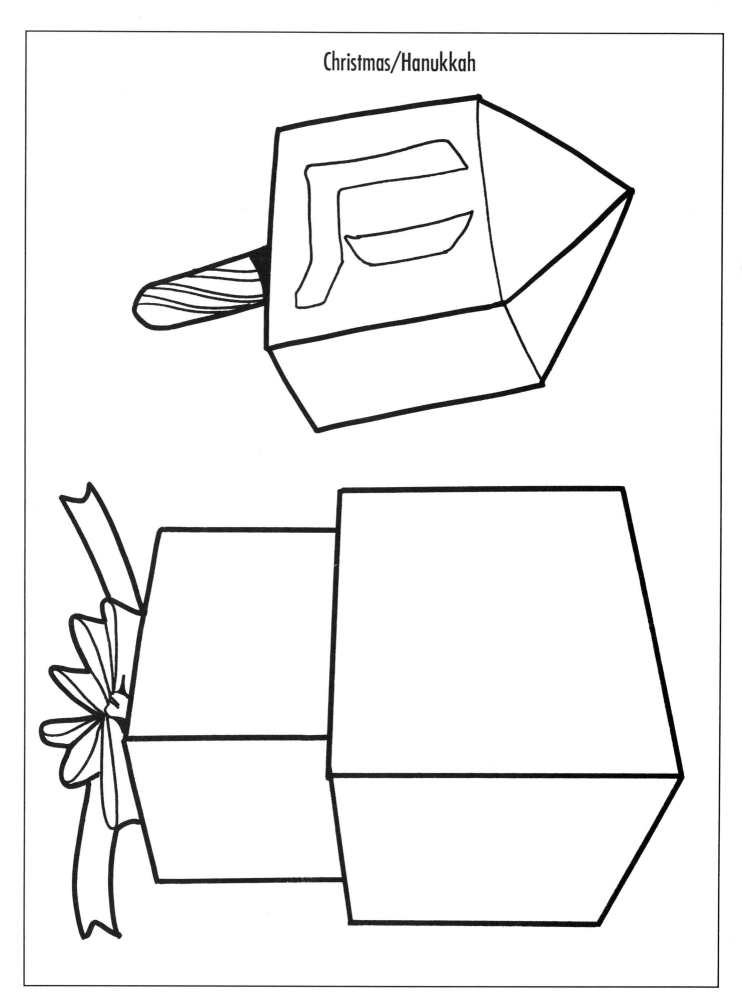

GA1341

GA1341

GA1341

Christmas/Hanukkah

GA1341

GA1341

GA1341

SEEDS

GA1341

Spring Patterns

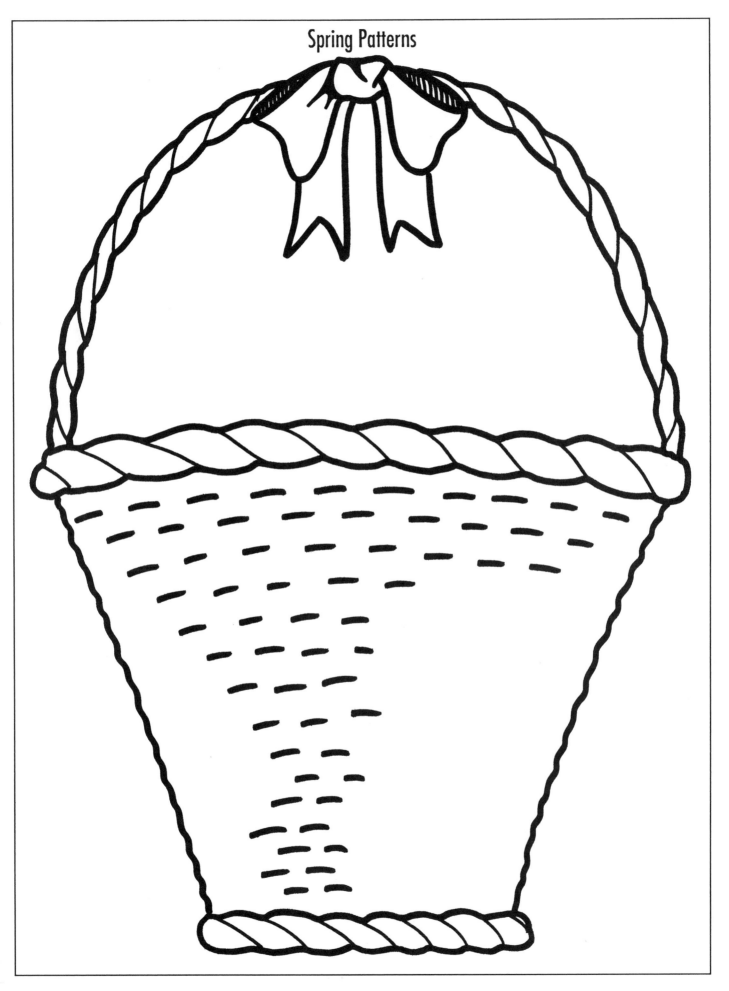

67

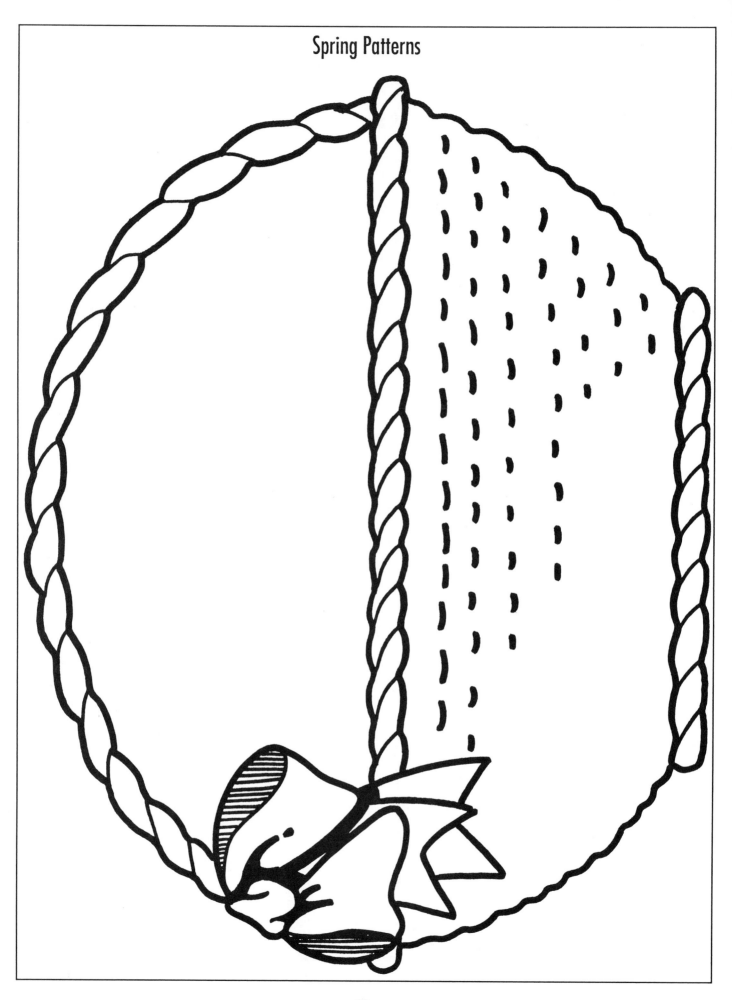

68

Spring Patterns

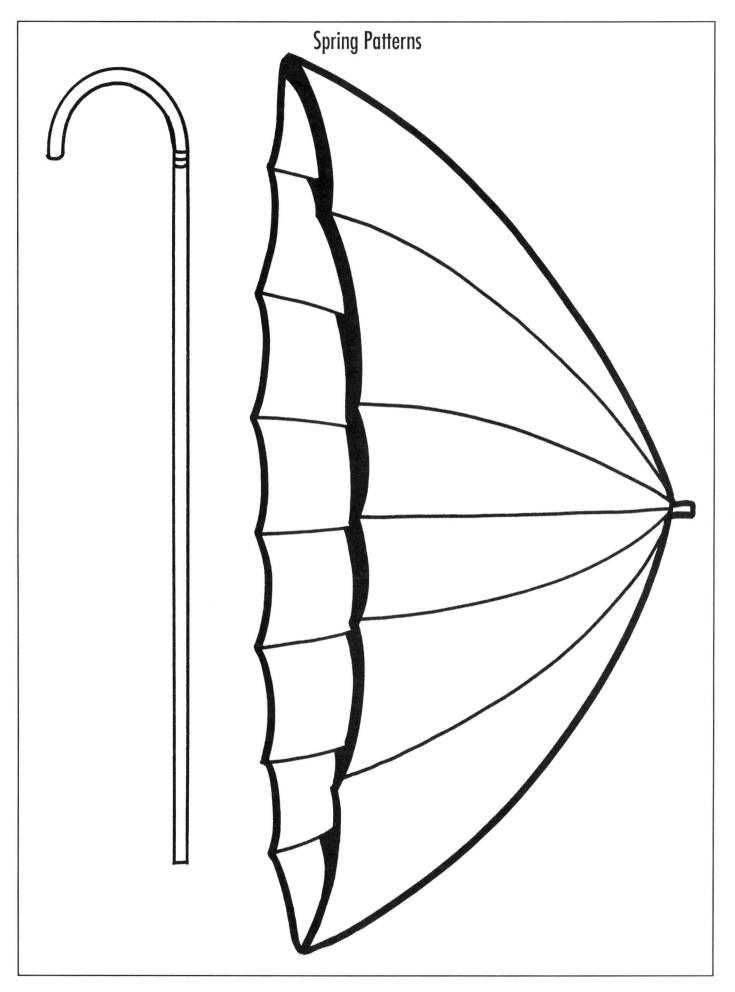

69

GA1341

71

GA1341

Spring Patterns

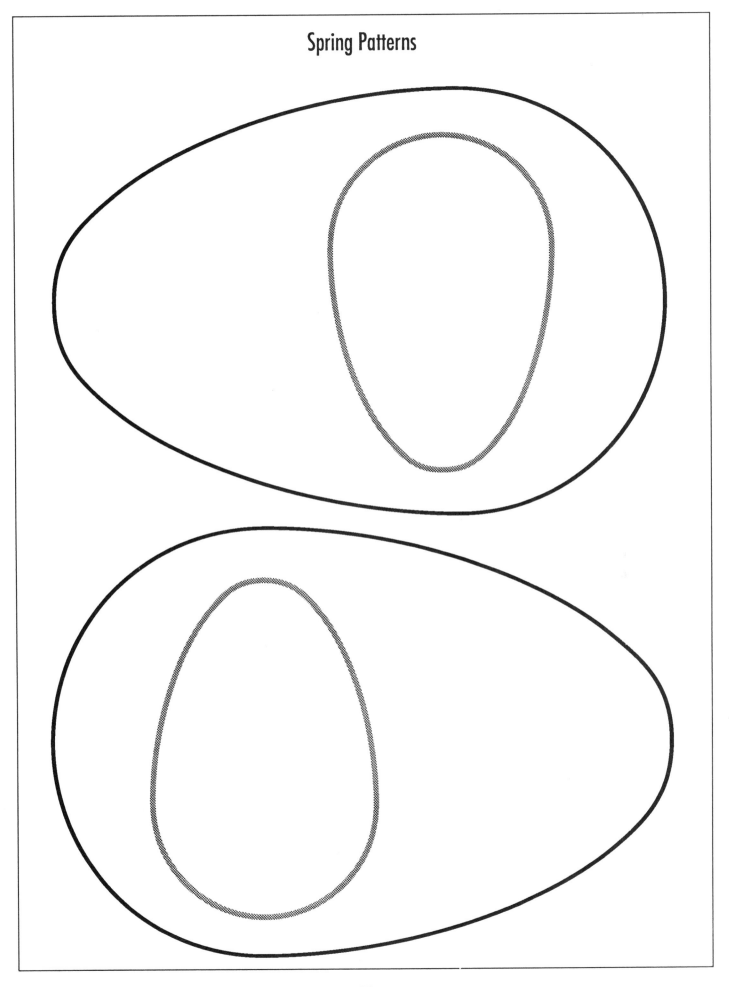

GA1341

Spring Patterns

GA1341

GA1341

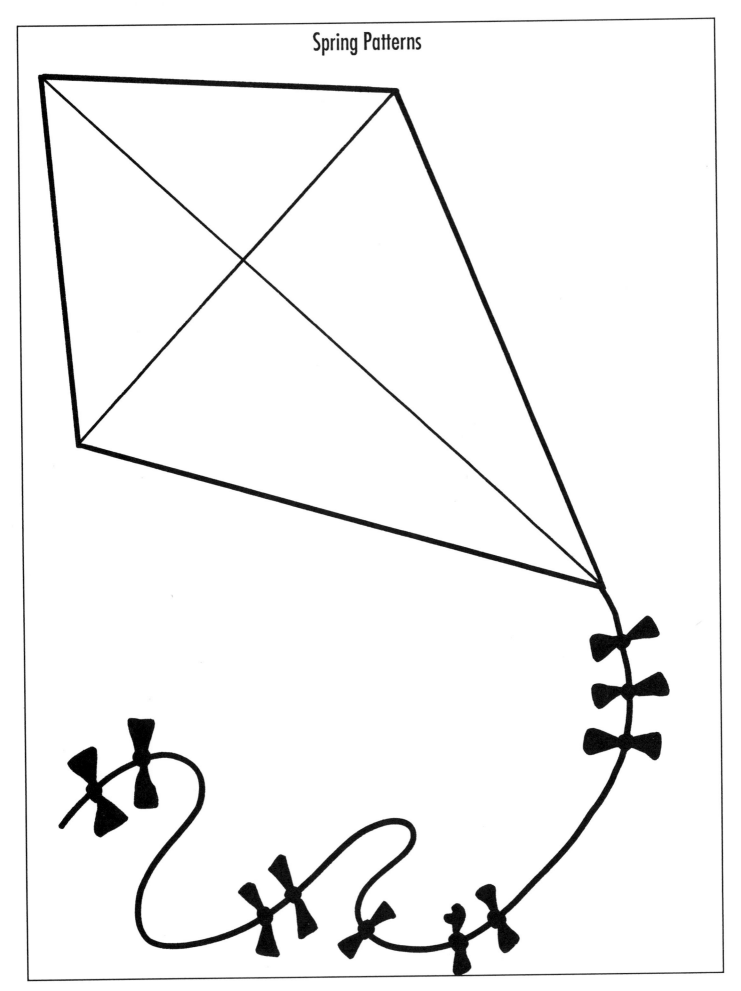

77

GA1341

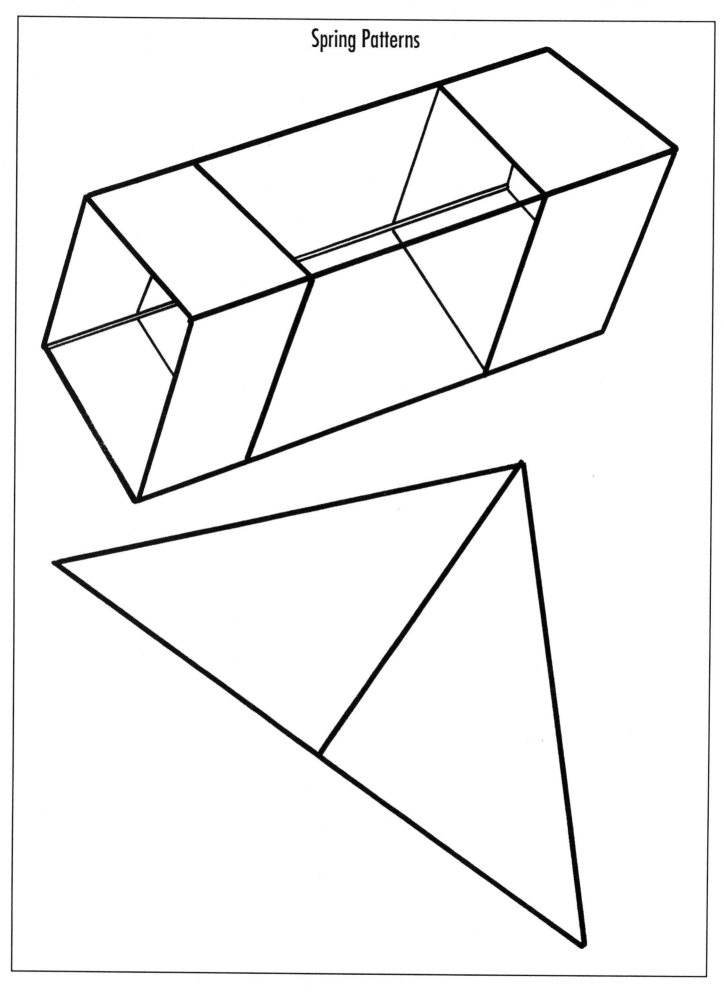

GA1341

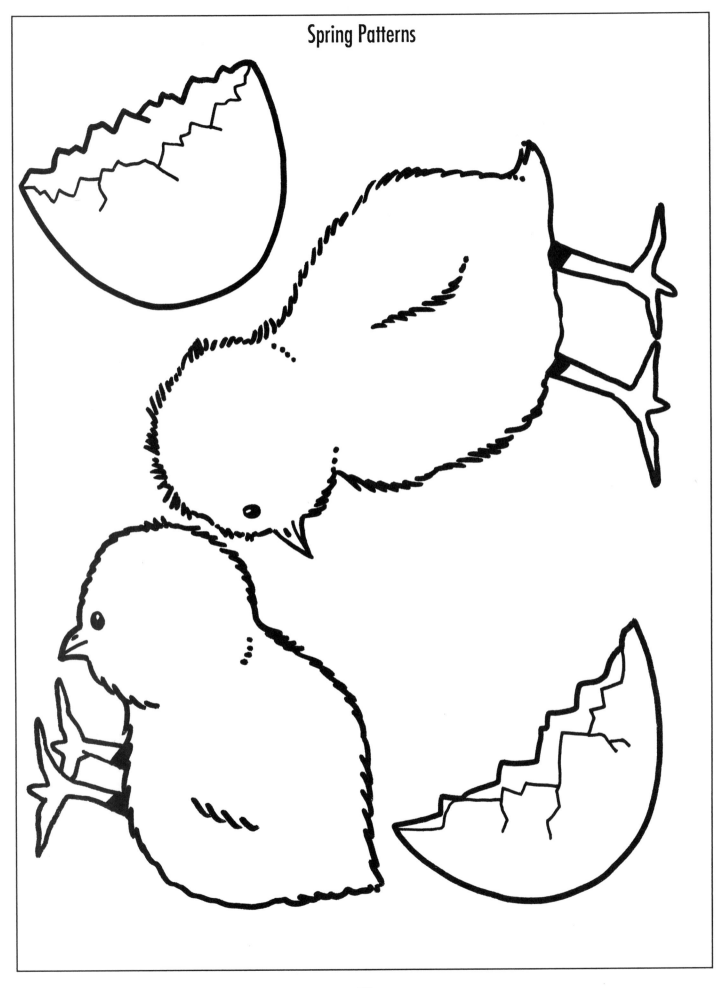

GA1341

GA1341

GA1341

Saint Patrick's Day

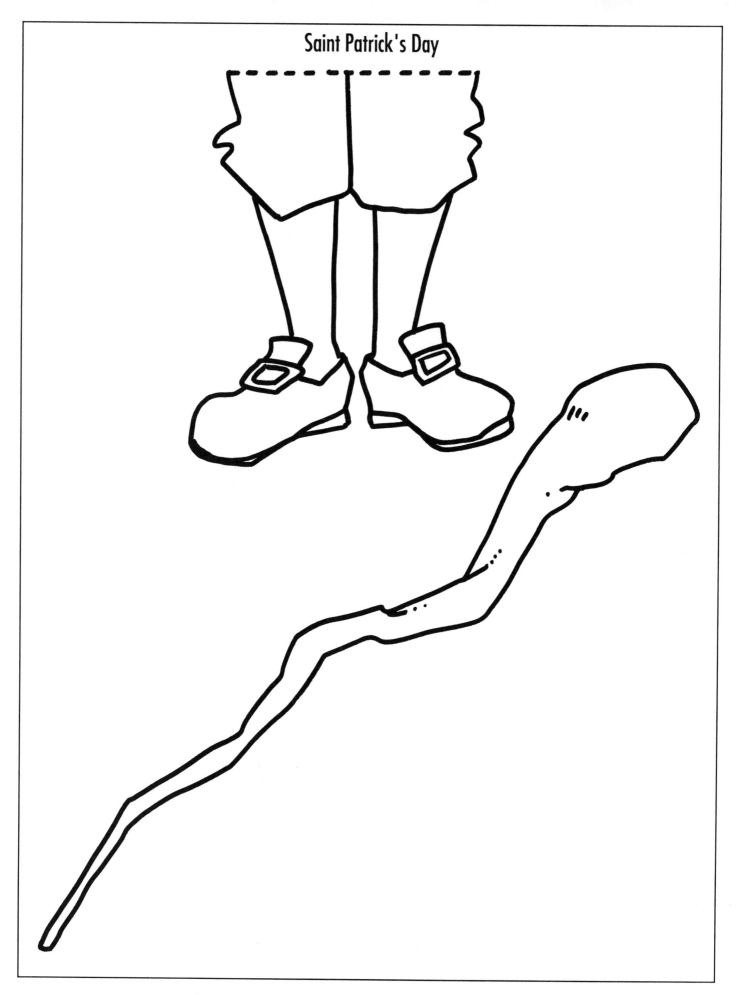

82

GA1341

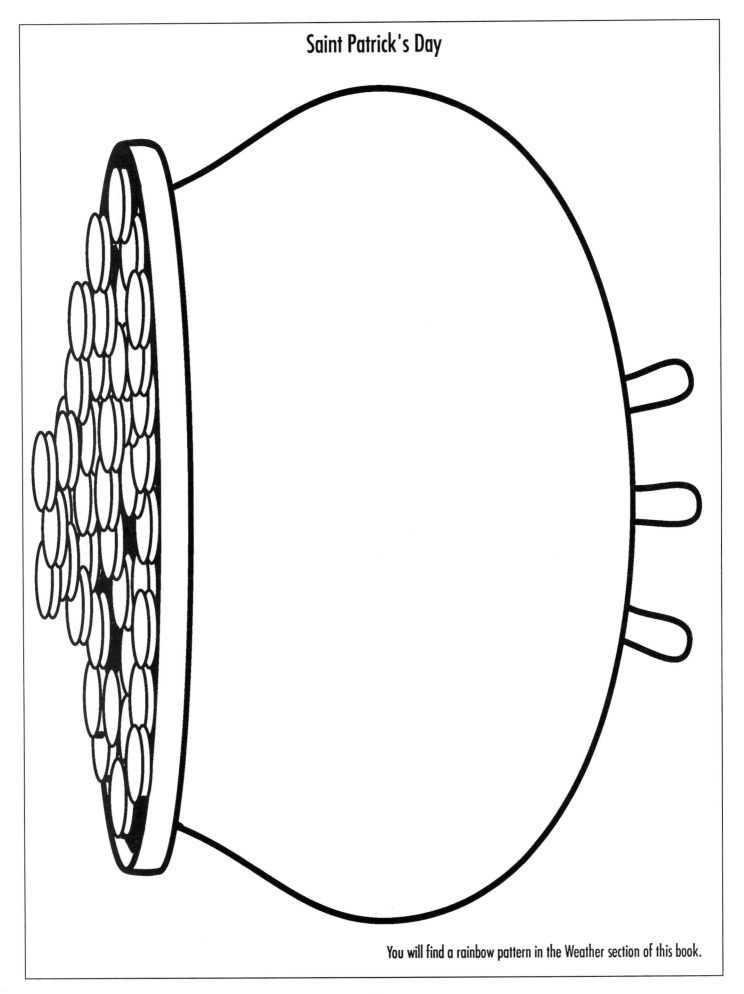

You will find a rainbow pattern in the Weather section of this book.

GA1341

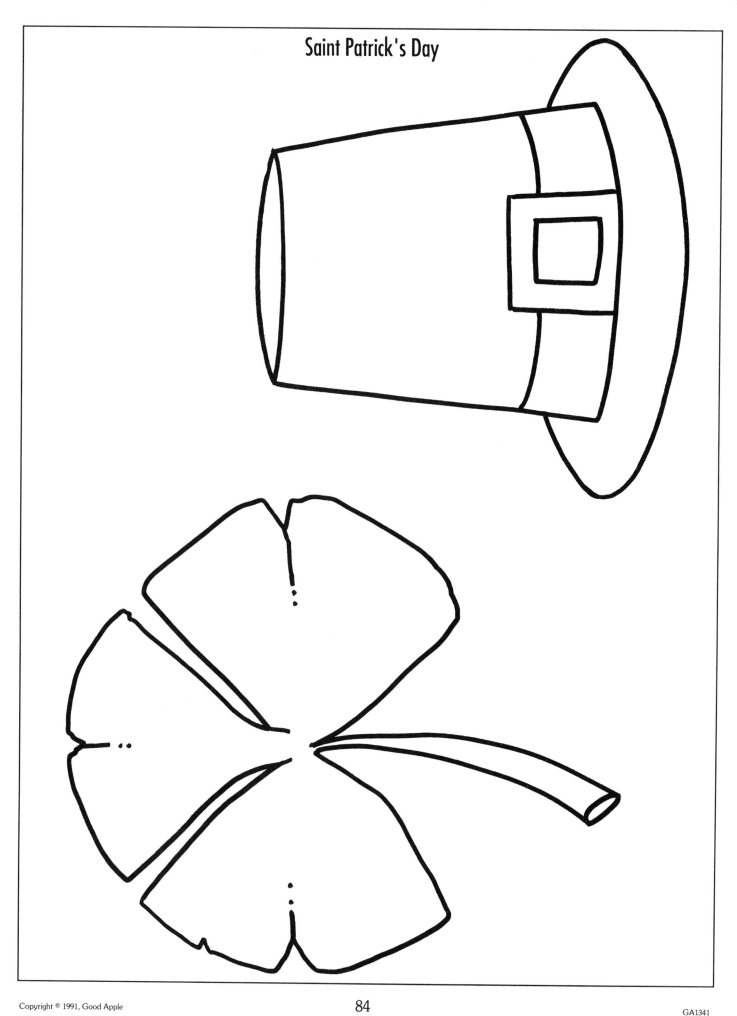

GA1341

Graduation

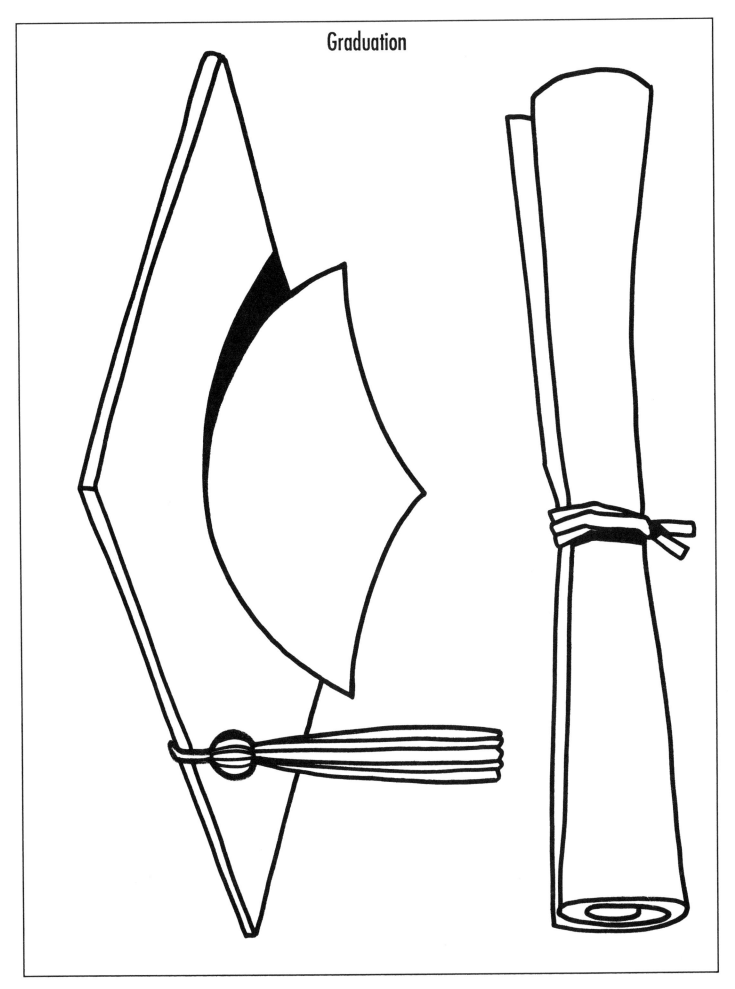

GA1341

Diploma

This is to certify that _____

has completed _____

Date _____

Signed _____

GA1341

Summer Patterns

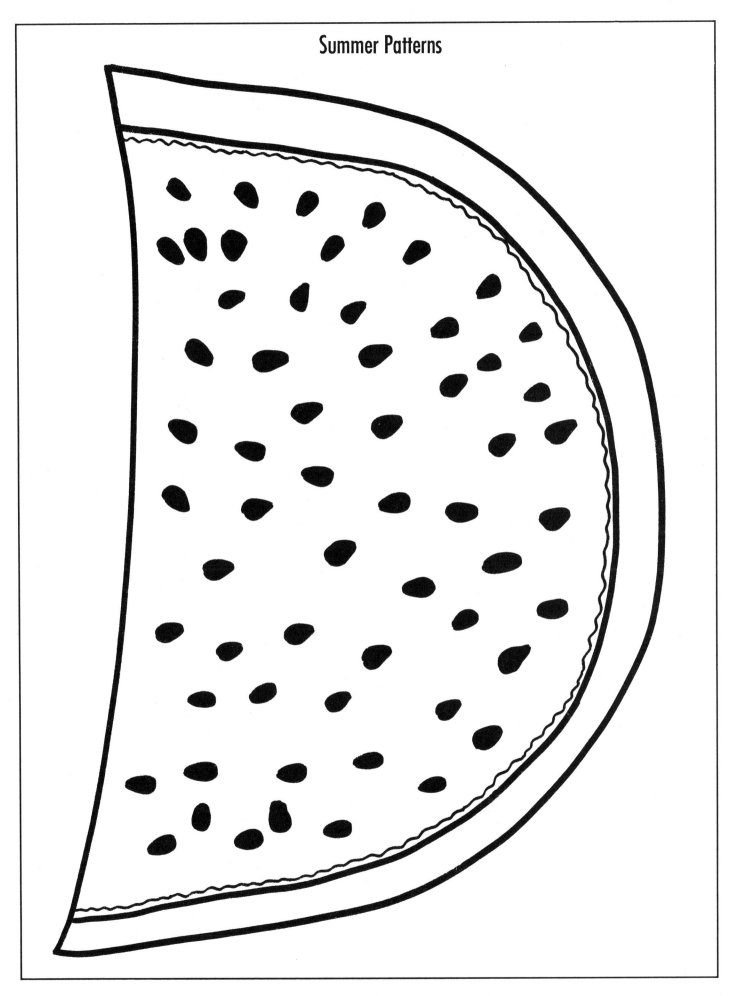

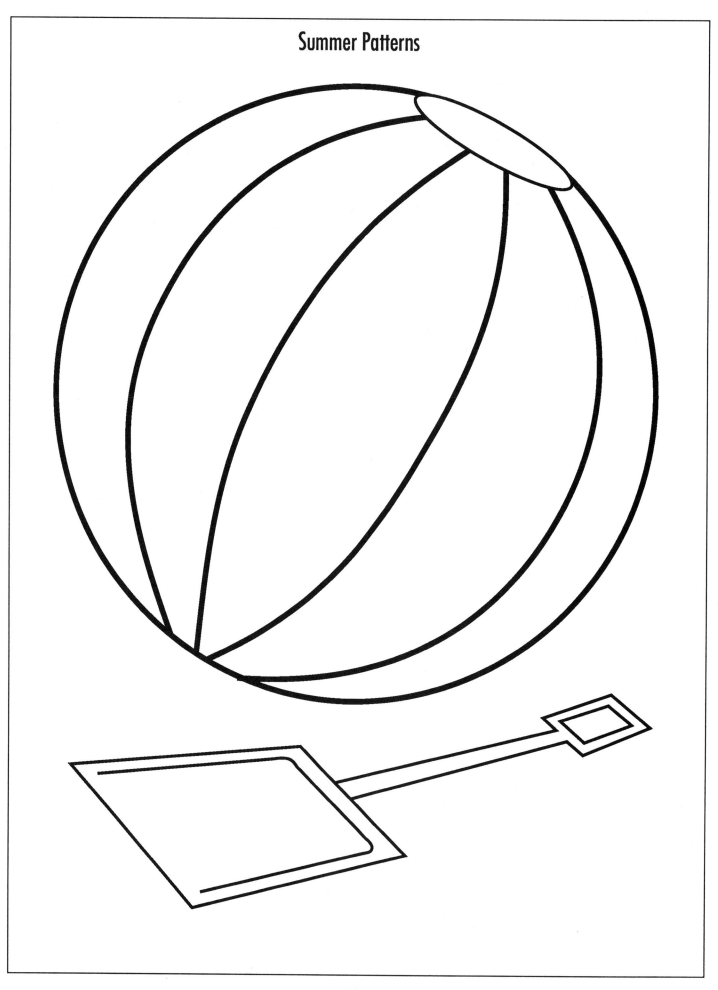

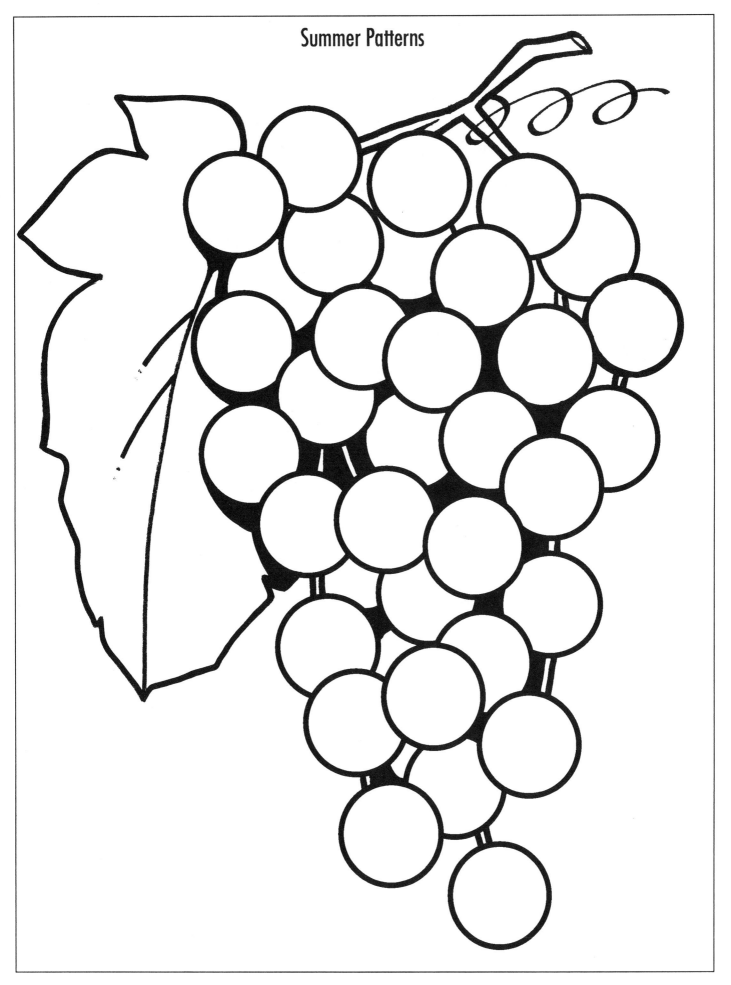

GA1341

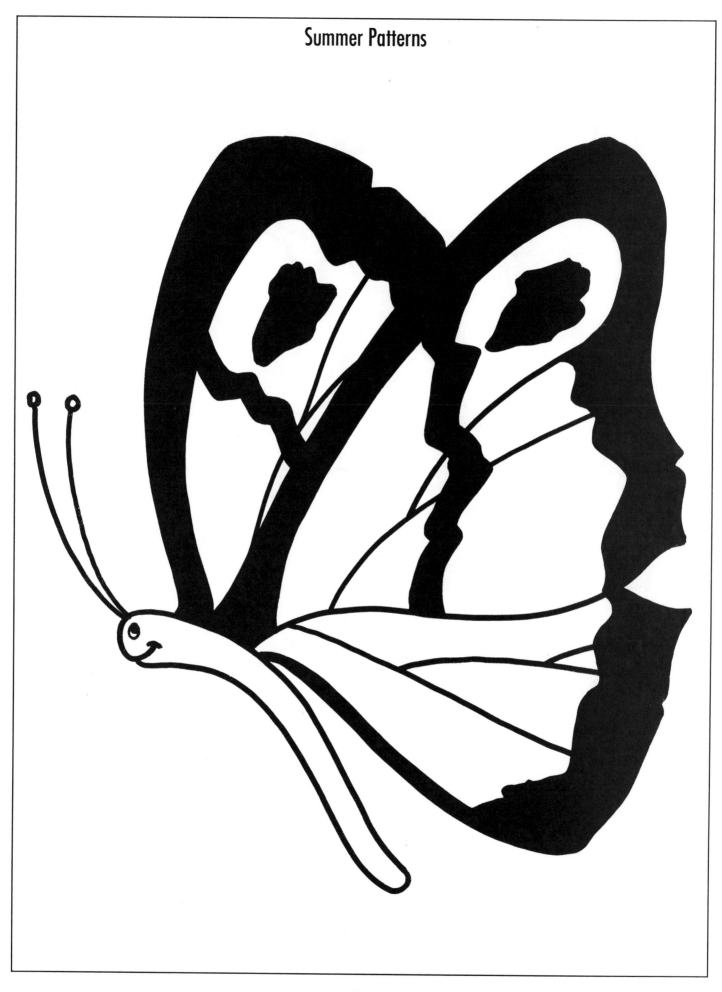

GA1341

Trees for hammock
are found on the
following page.

GA1341

GA1341

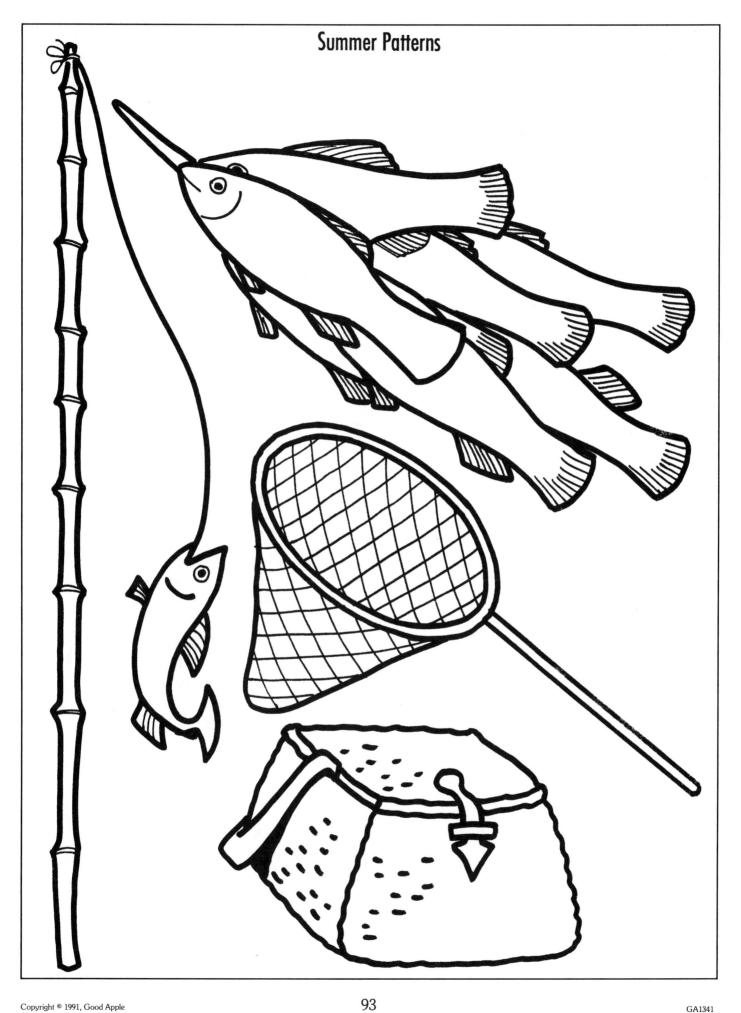

GA1341

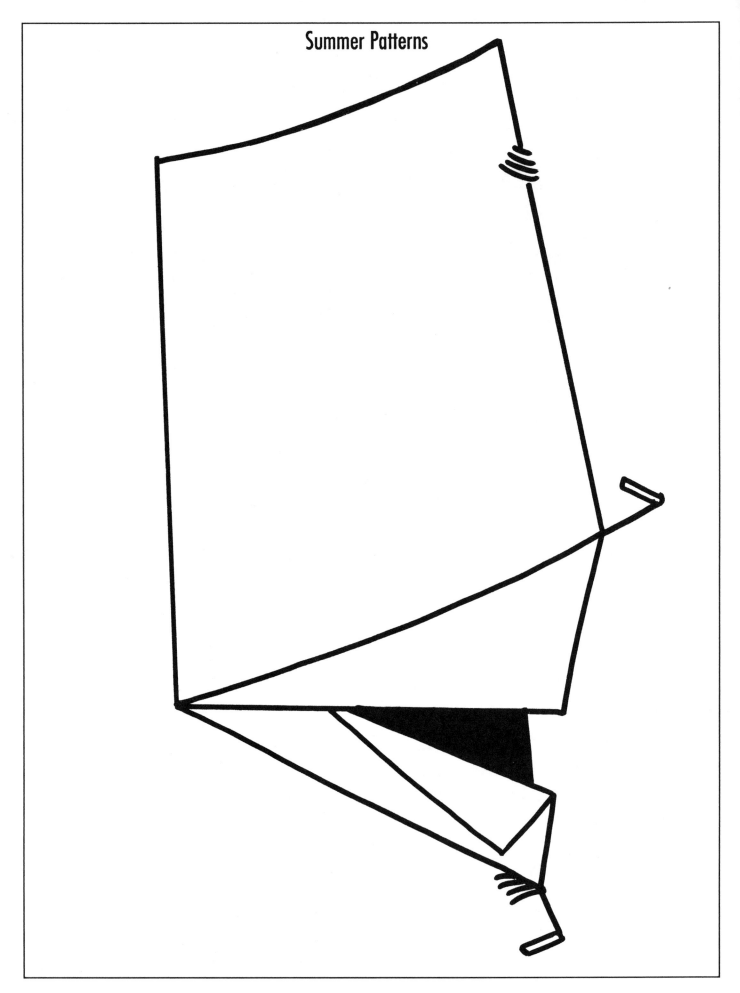

GA1341

97

GA1341

GA1341

GA1341

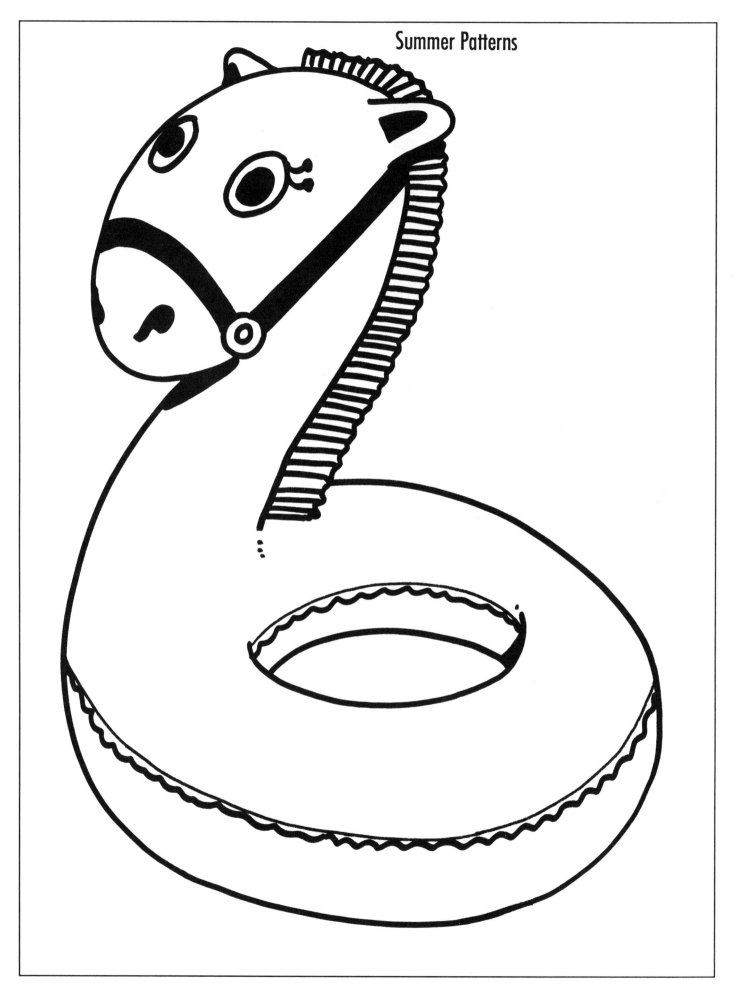

101

GA1341

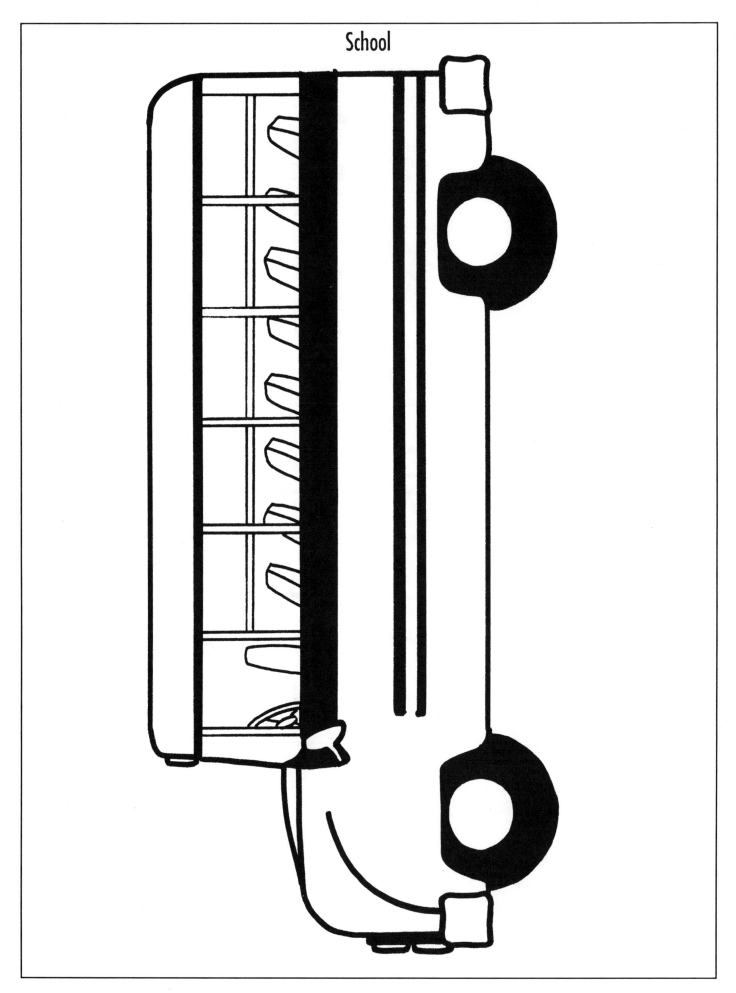

102

GA1341

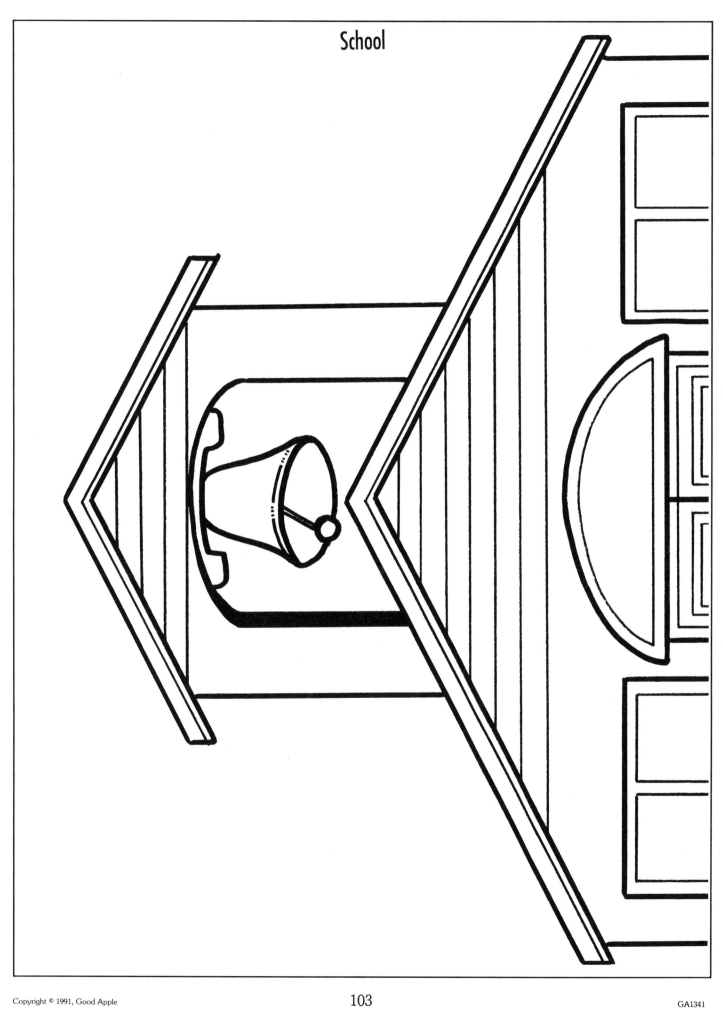

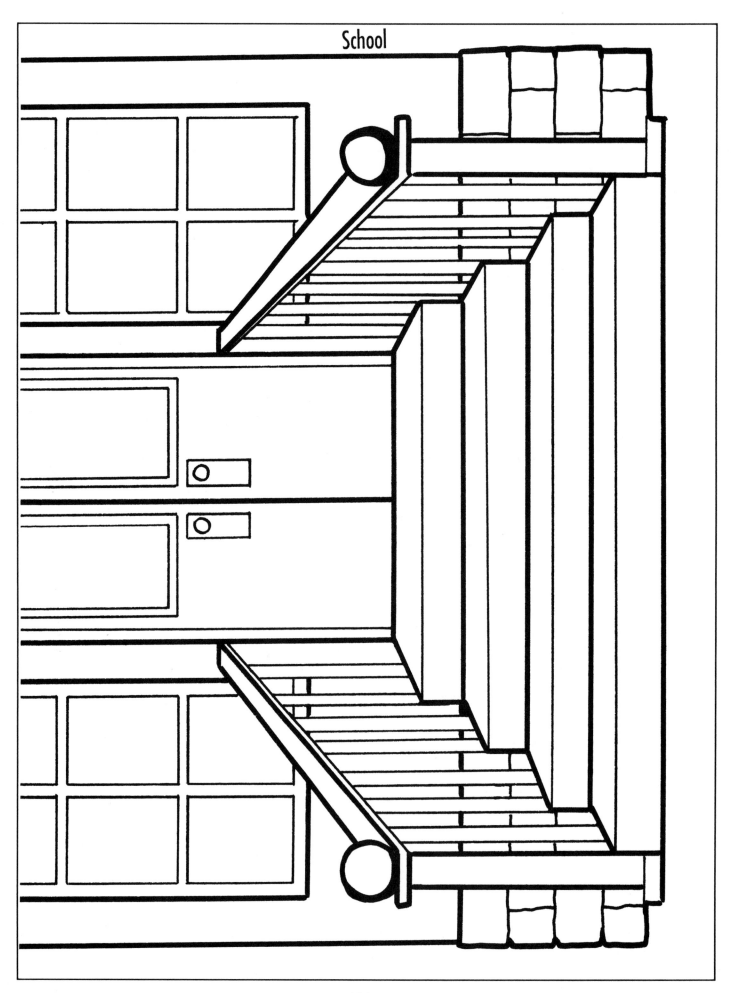

GA1341

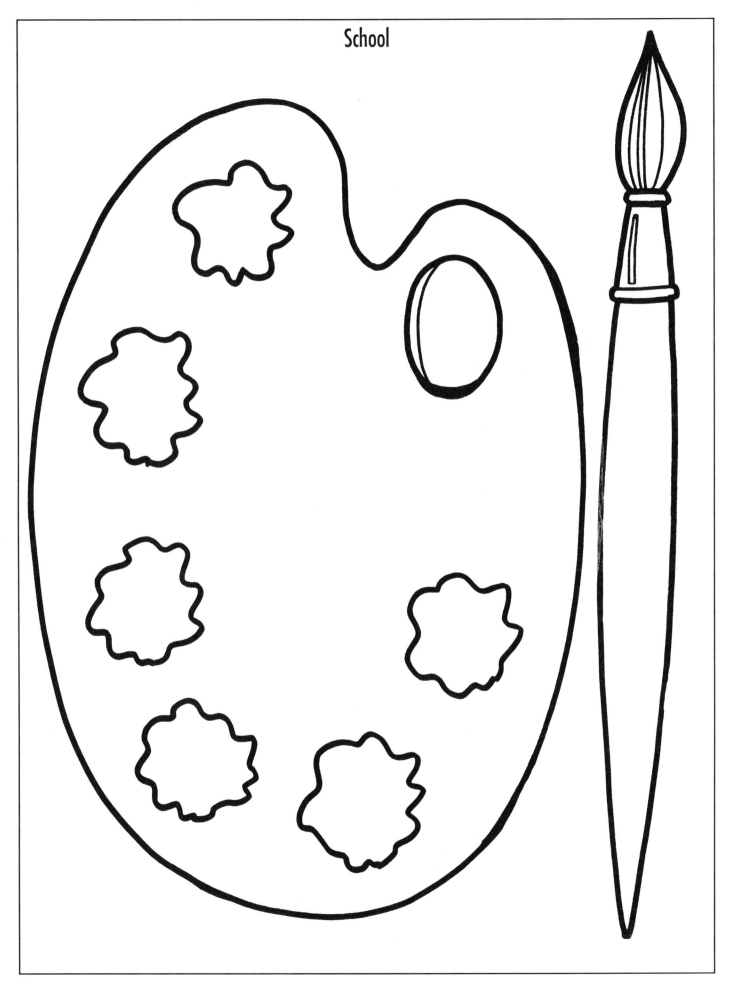

glue

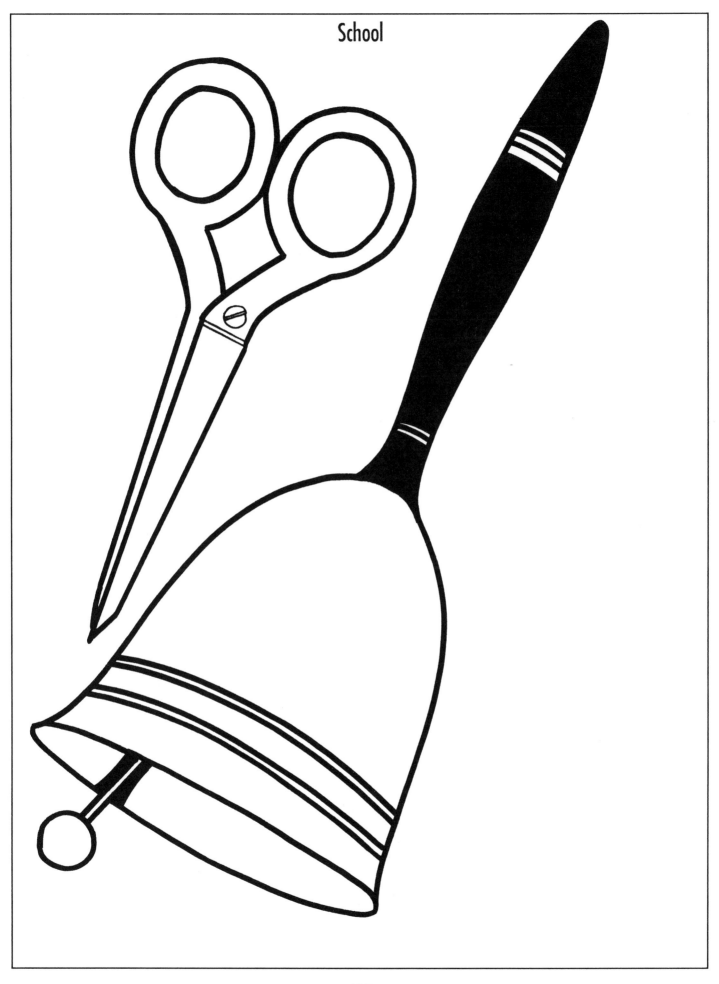

GA1341

108

GA1341

GA1341

GA1341

School

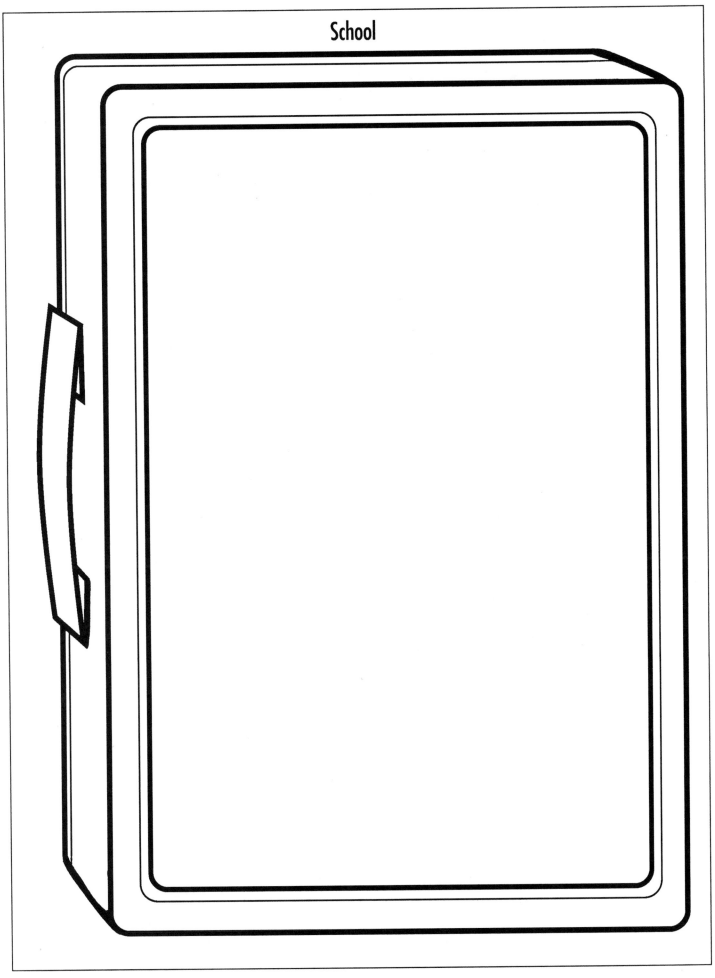

GA1341

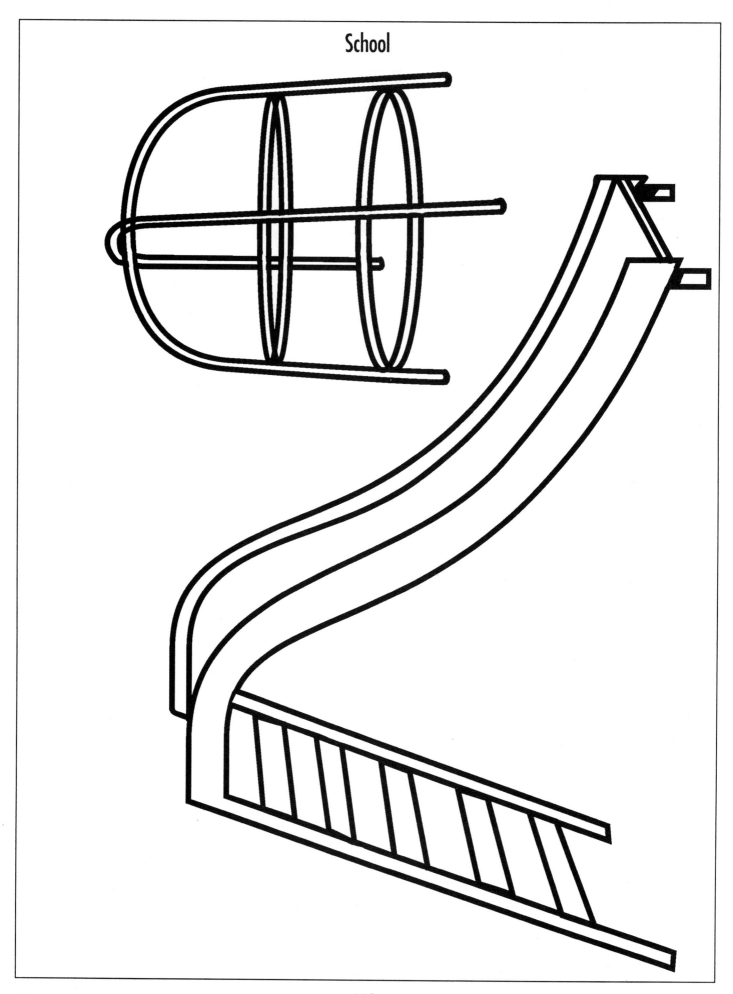

GA1341

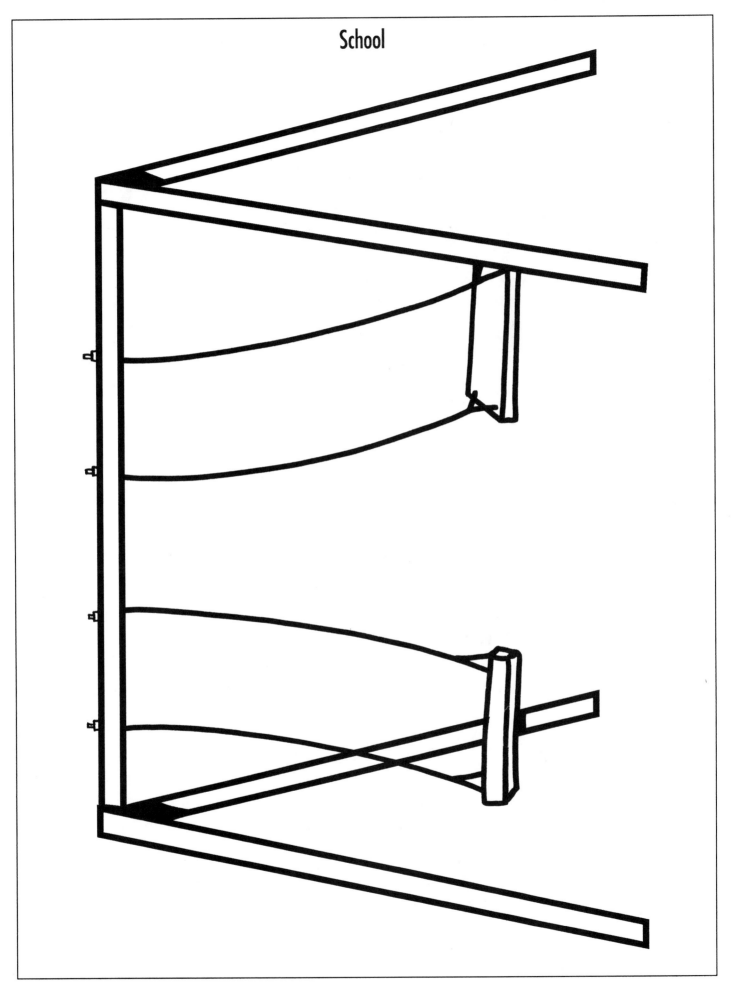

113

GA1341

GA1341

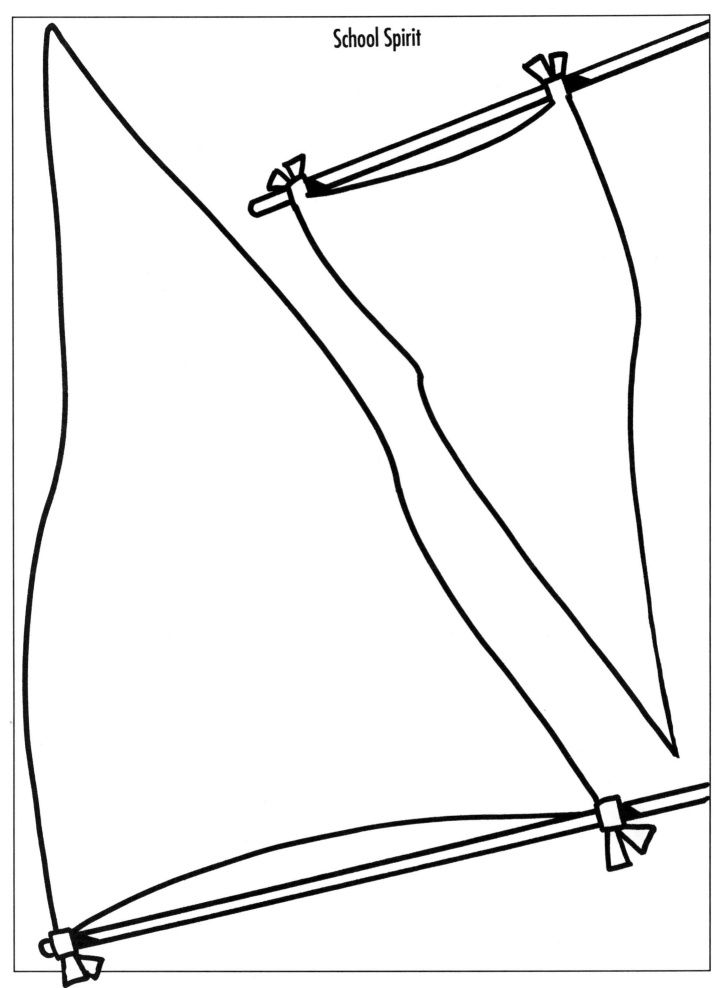

115

GA1341

Sports

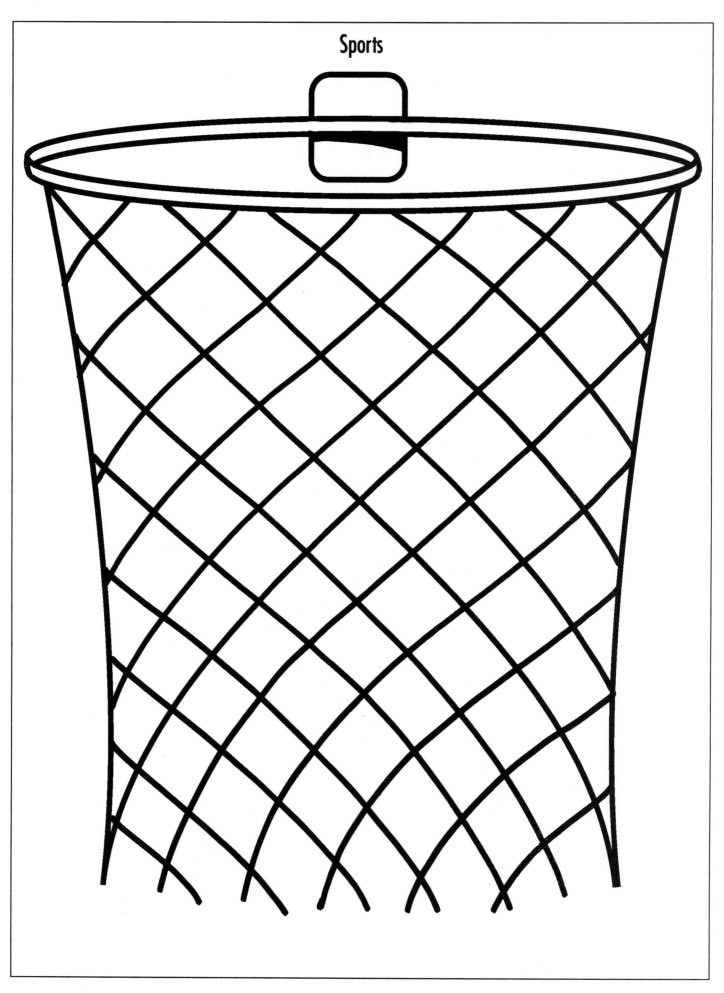

118

Sports

120

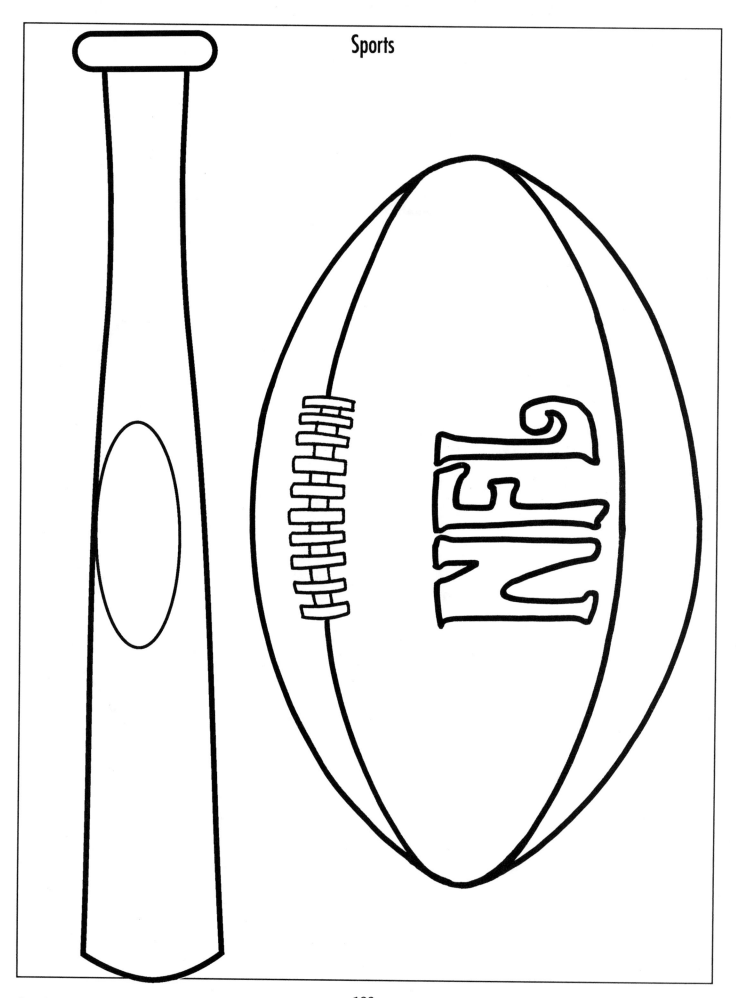

GA1341

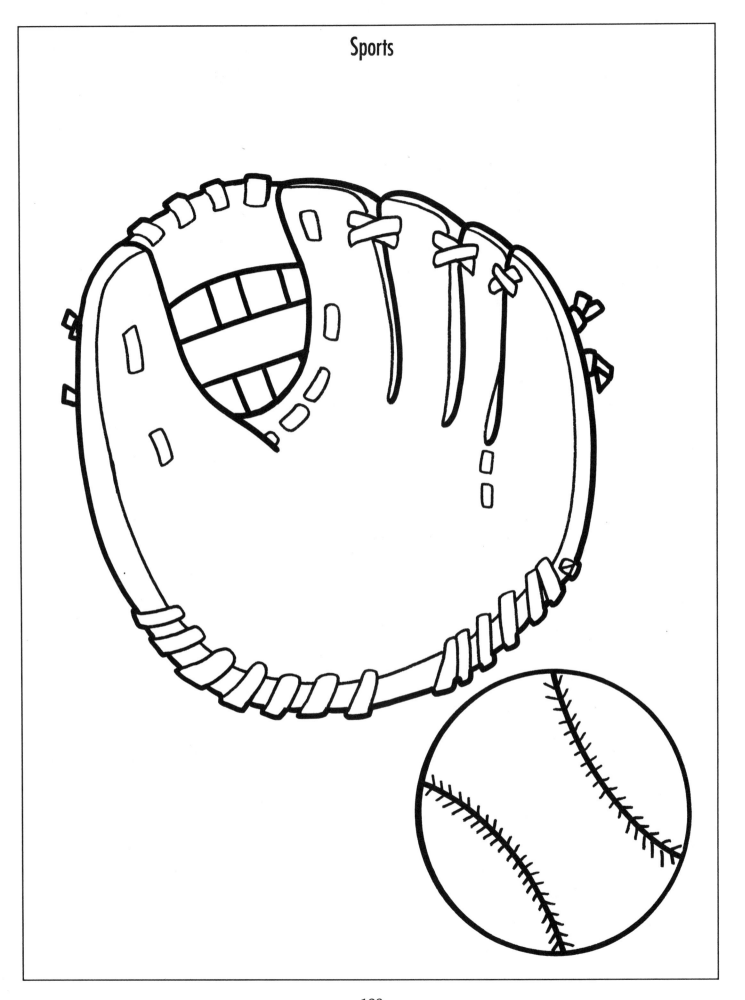

GA1341

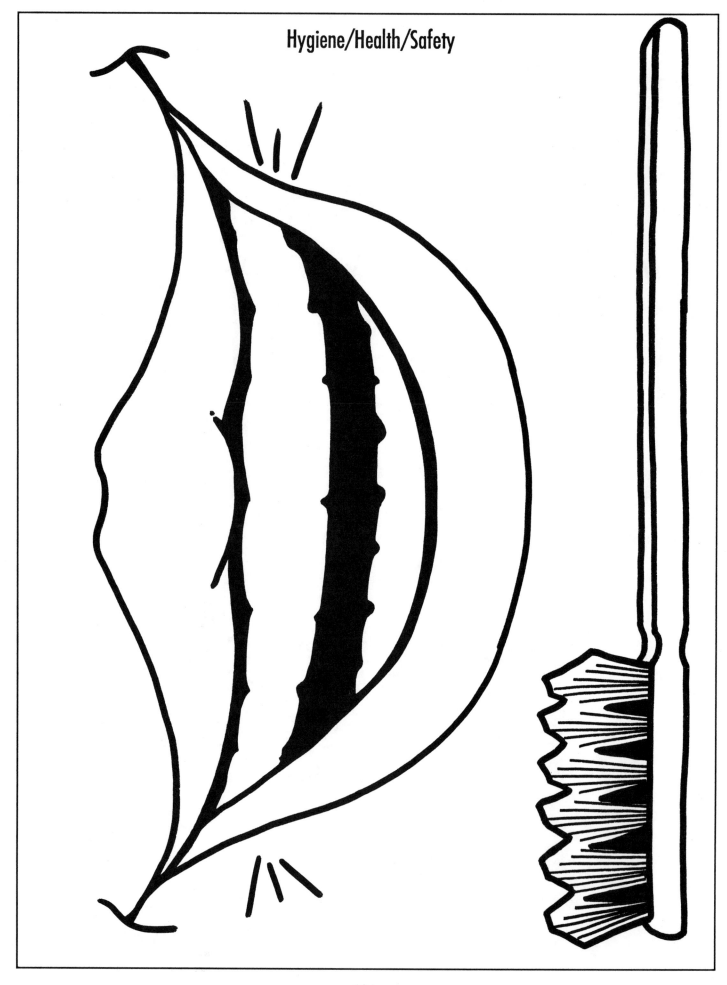

GA1341

 GA1341

126

GA1341

Family

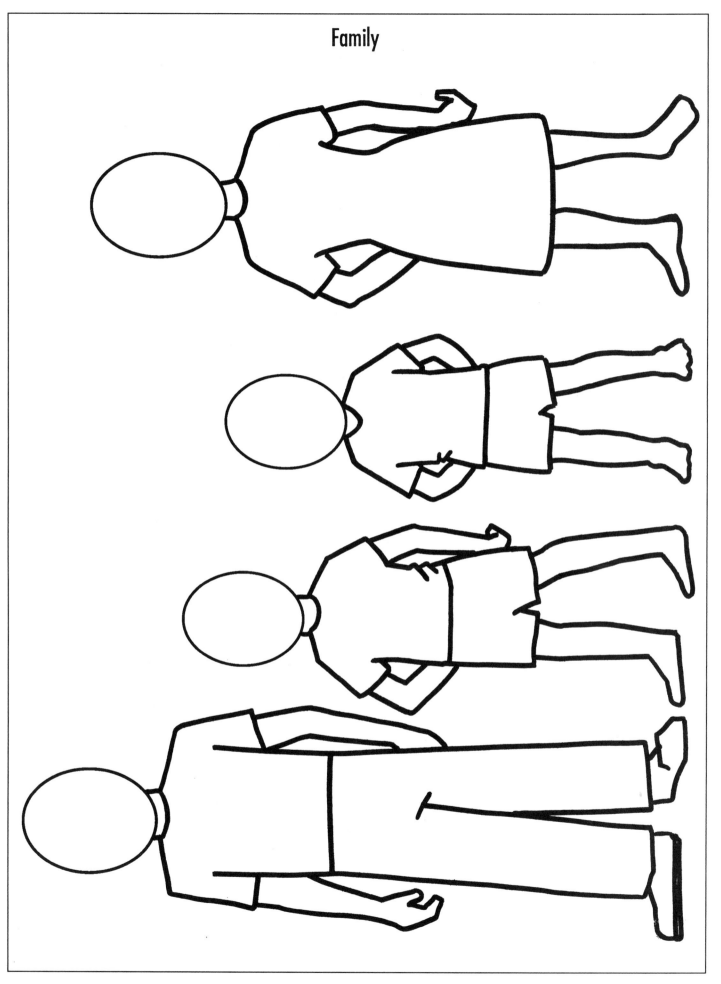

127

GA1341

All Kinds of Faces

You can use these faces by cutting on the dotted line and glueing them to other patterns found in this book. In this way you can add personality or "animation" to objects that are inanimate.

128

GA1341

130

GA1341

Spooky Letters

131

132

GA1341

134

GA1341

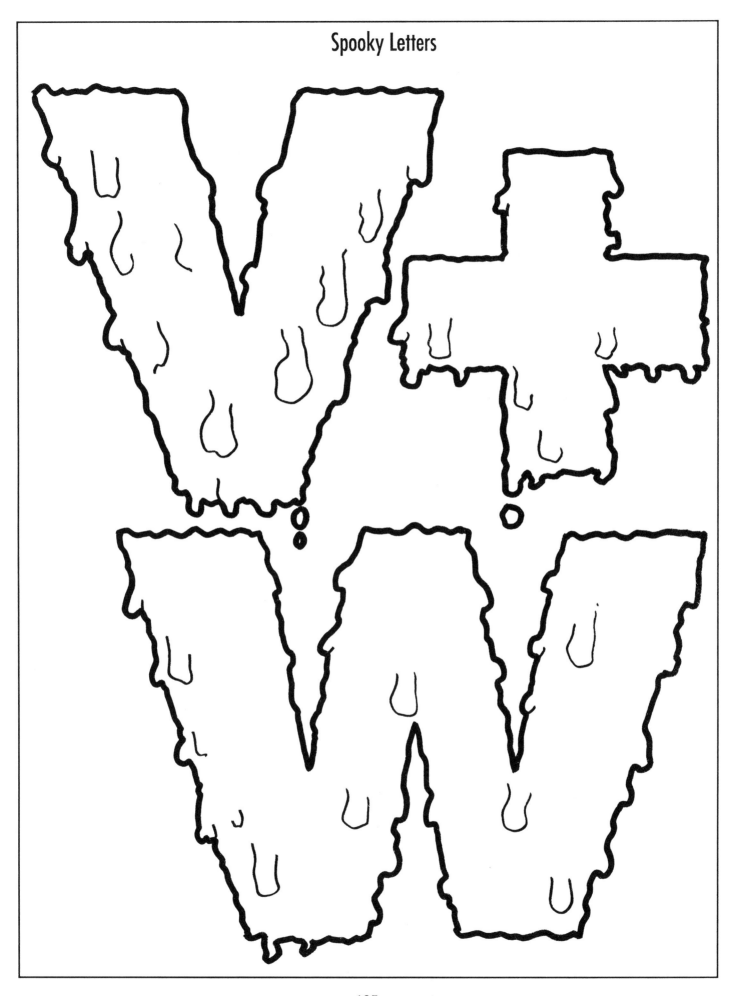

135

GA1341

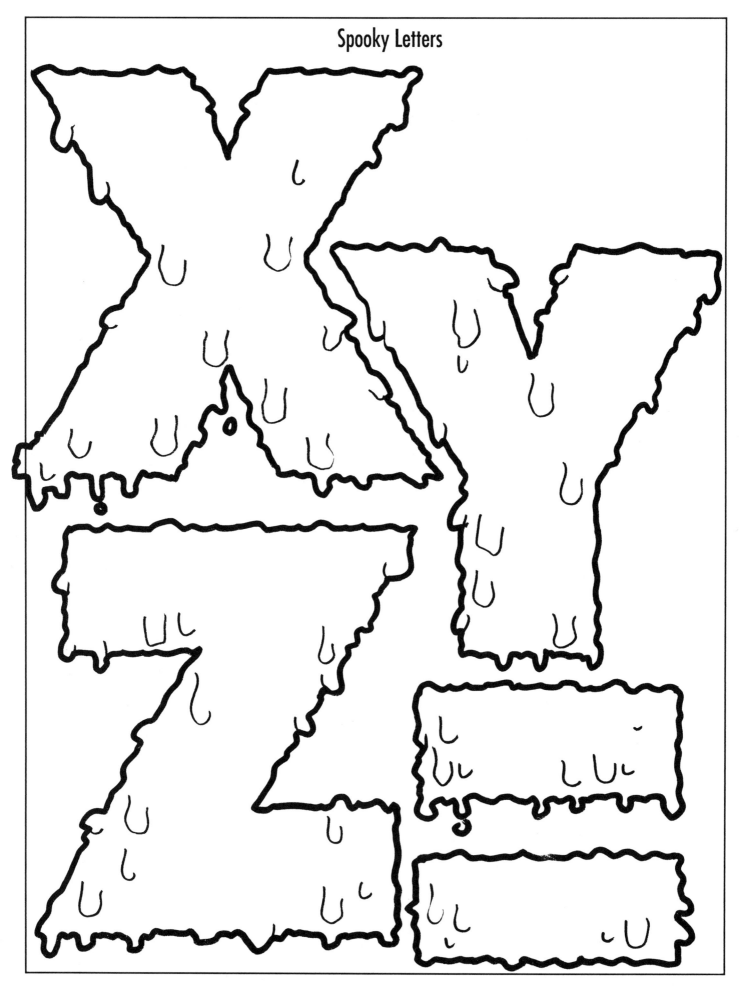

GA1341

GA1341

Spooky Numbers

GA1341

Spooky Numbers

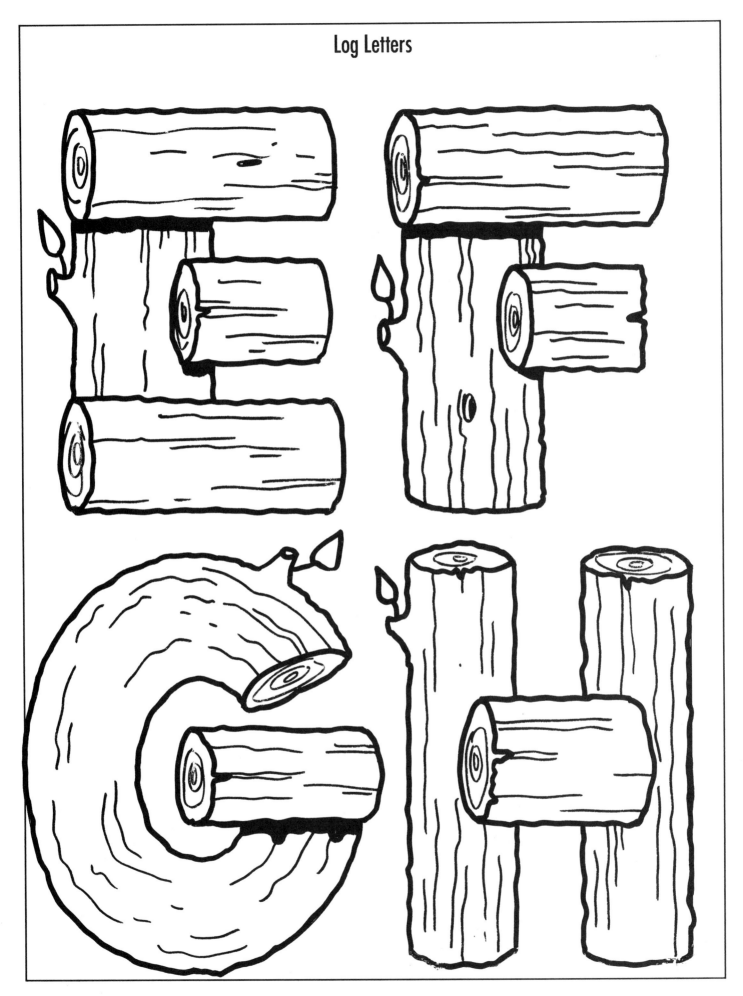

141

Log Letters

142

GA1341

143

GA1341

Log Letters

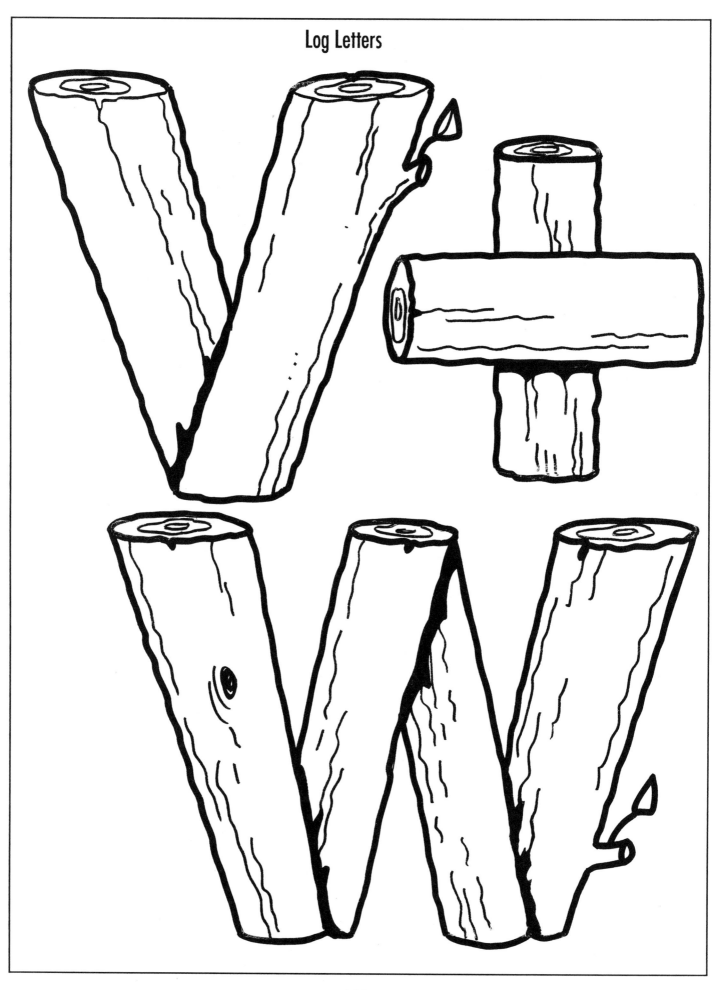

146

GA1341

Log Letters

GA1341

Log Numbers

GA1341

Log Numbers

GA1341

Log Numbers

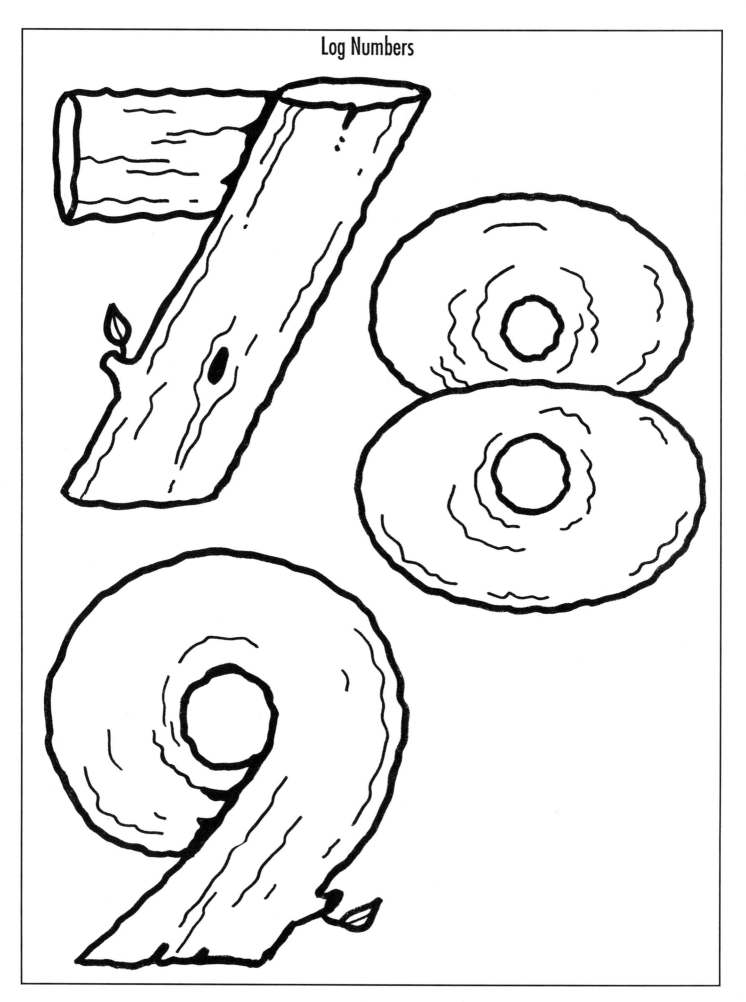

150

GA1341

151

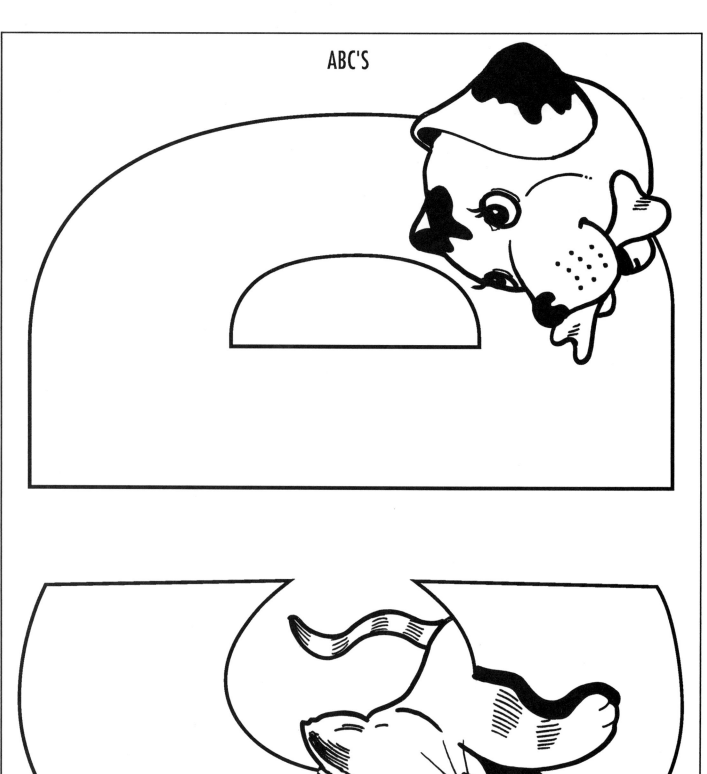

GA1341

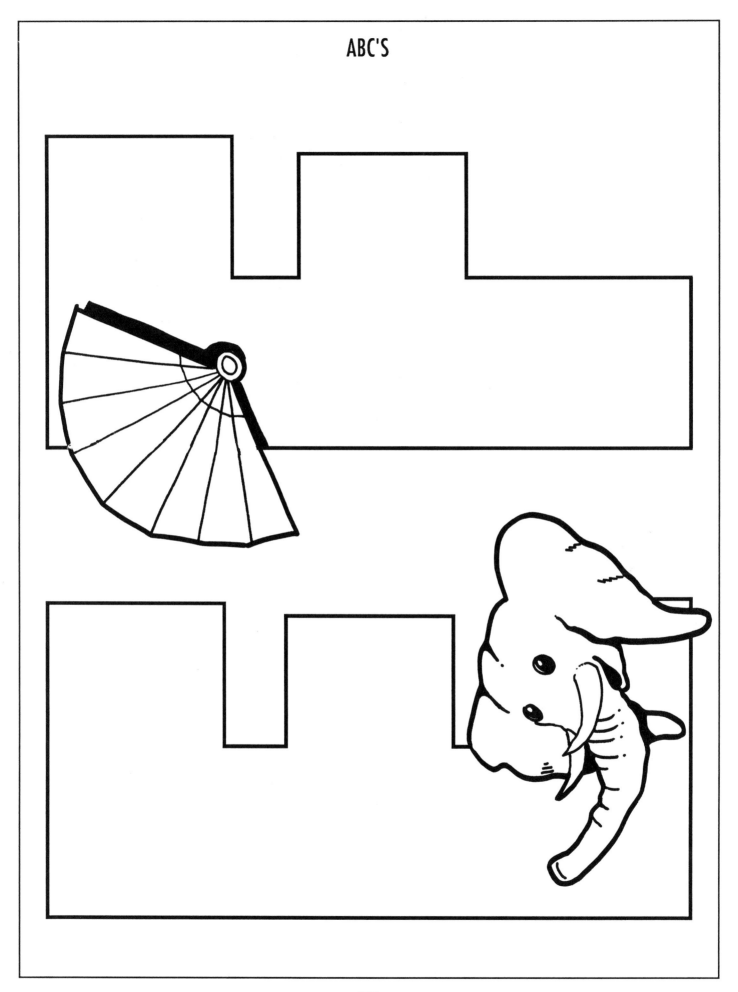

153

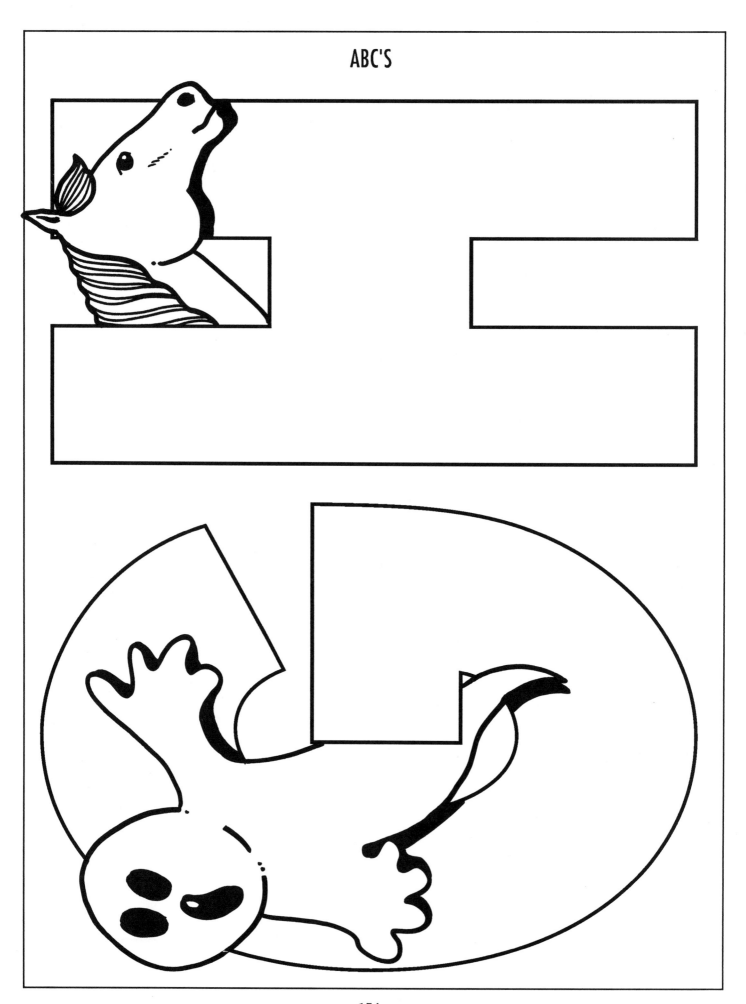

GA1341

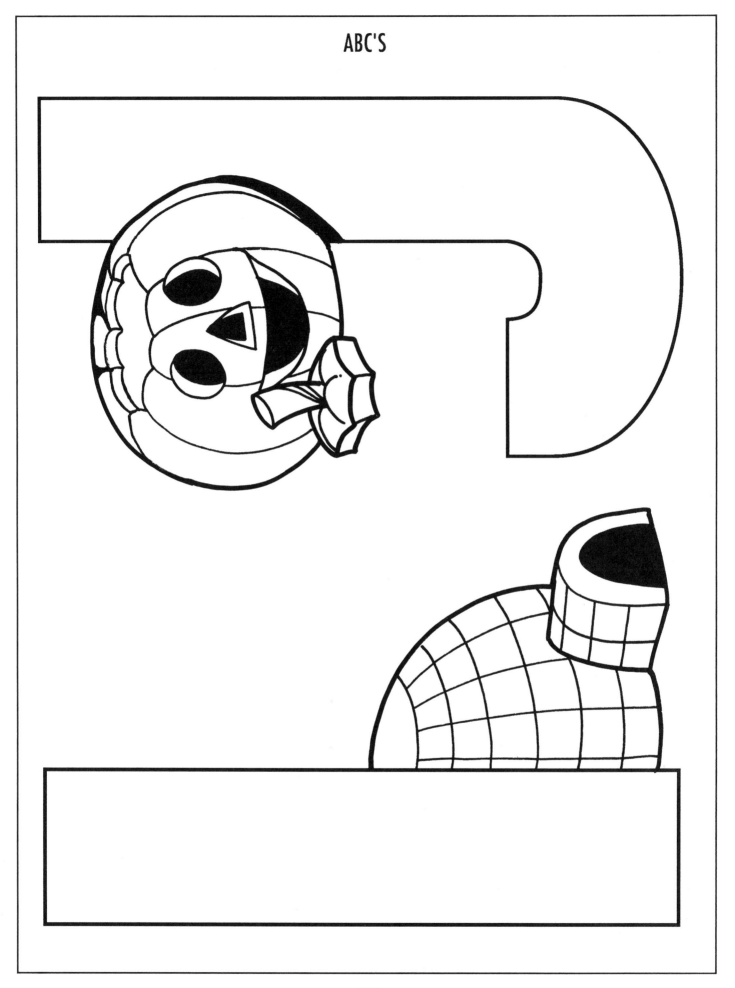

GA1341

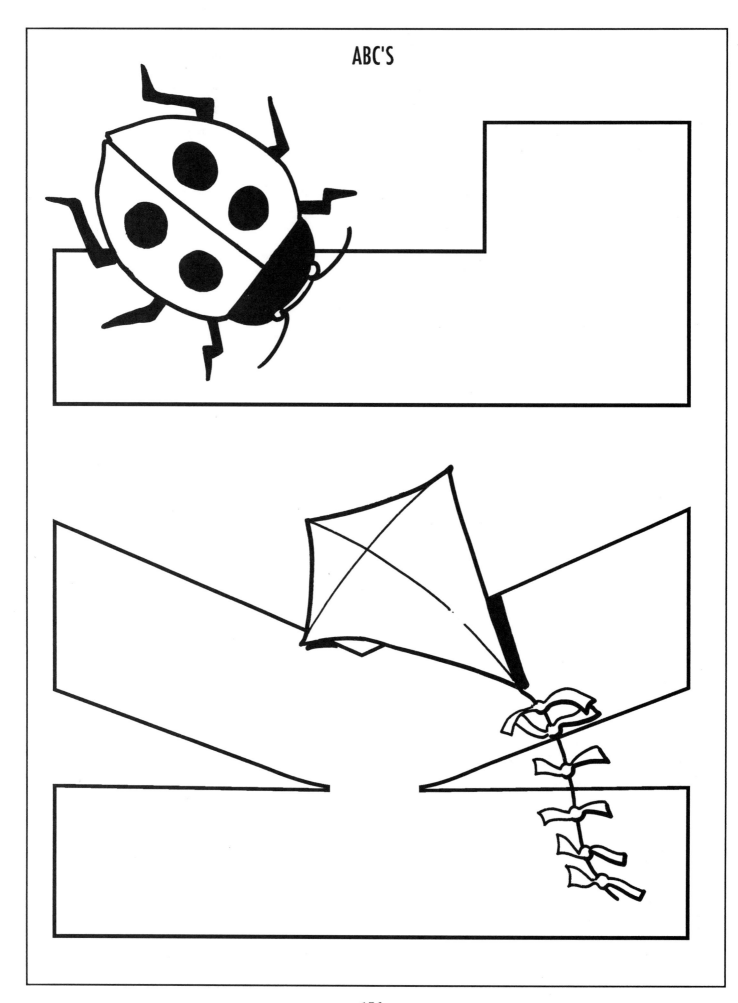

GA1341

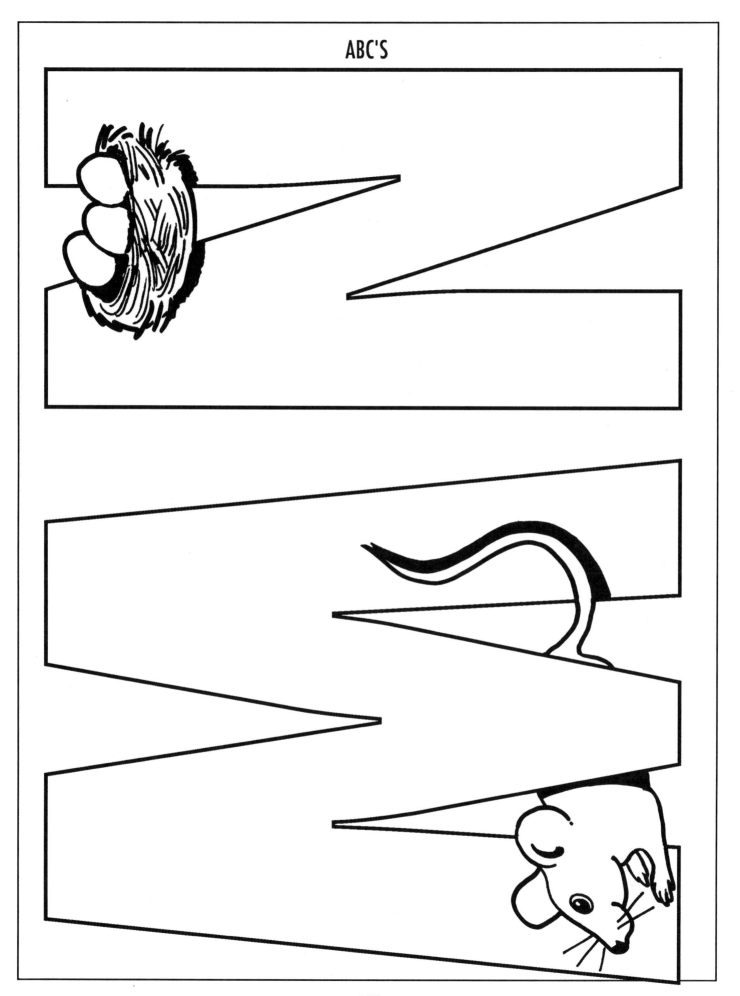

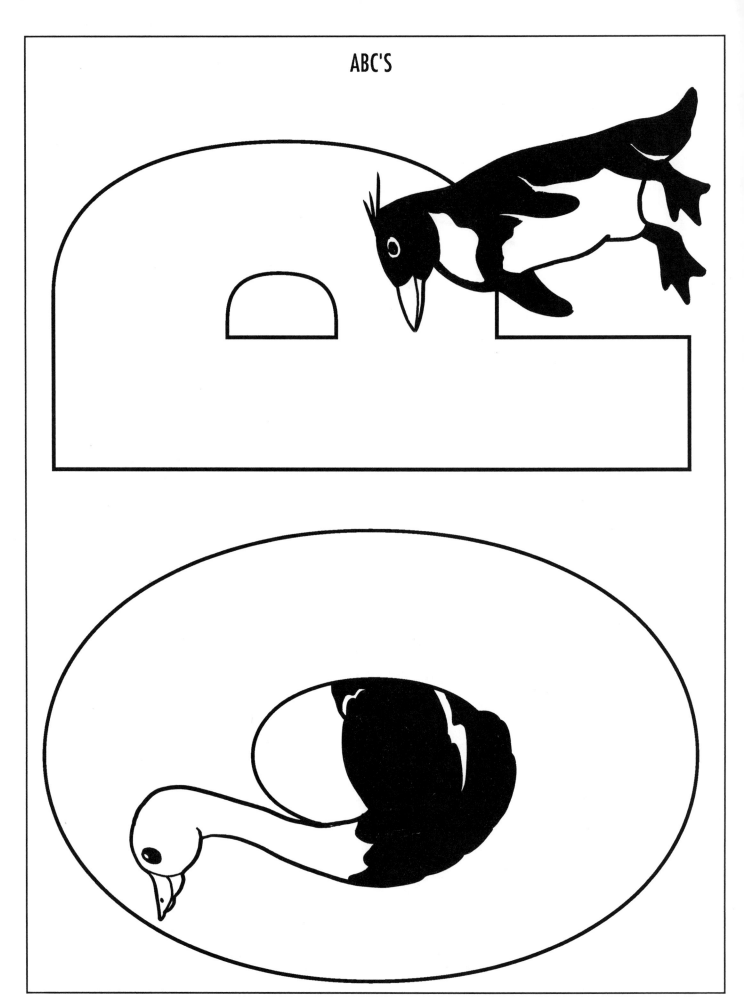

GA1341

ABC'S

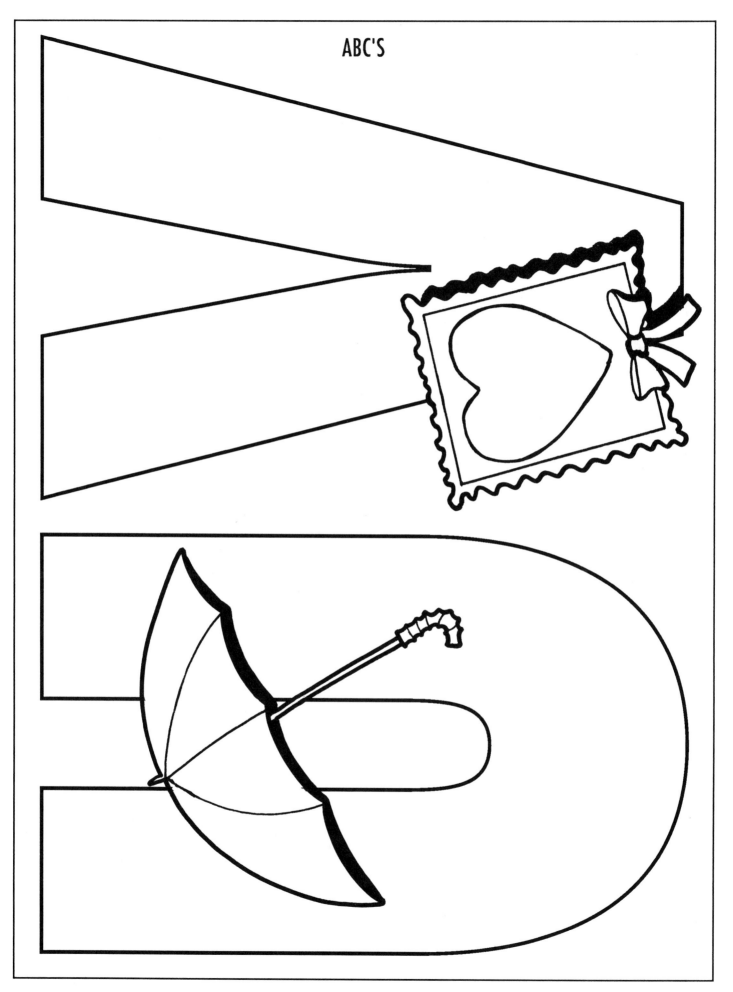

161

GA1341

ABC'S

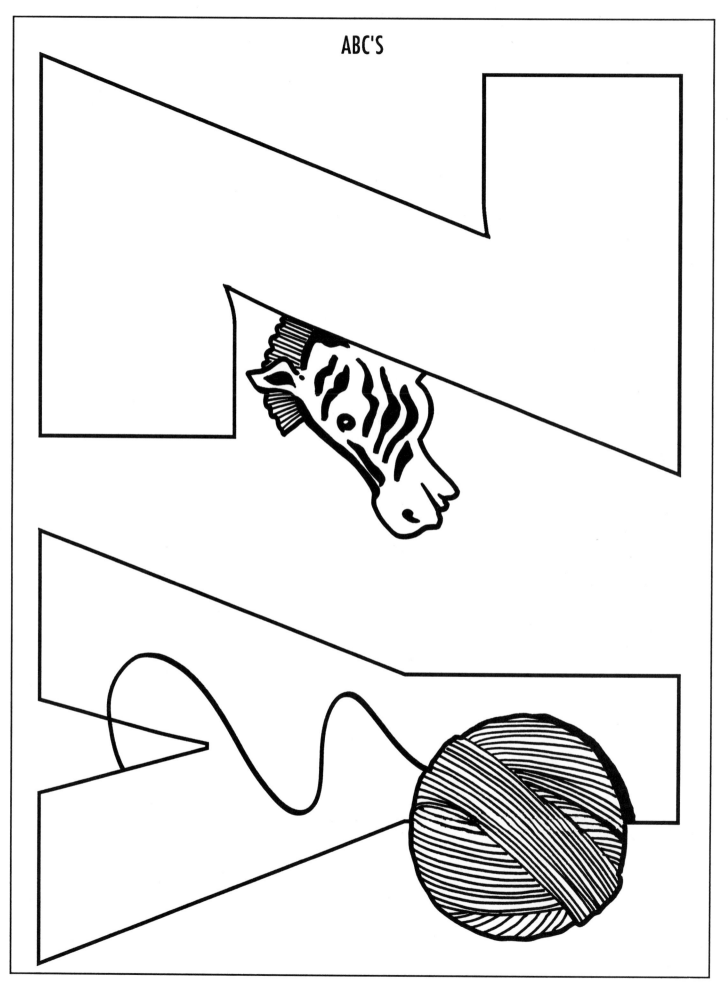

163

GA1341

Shapes

GA1341

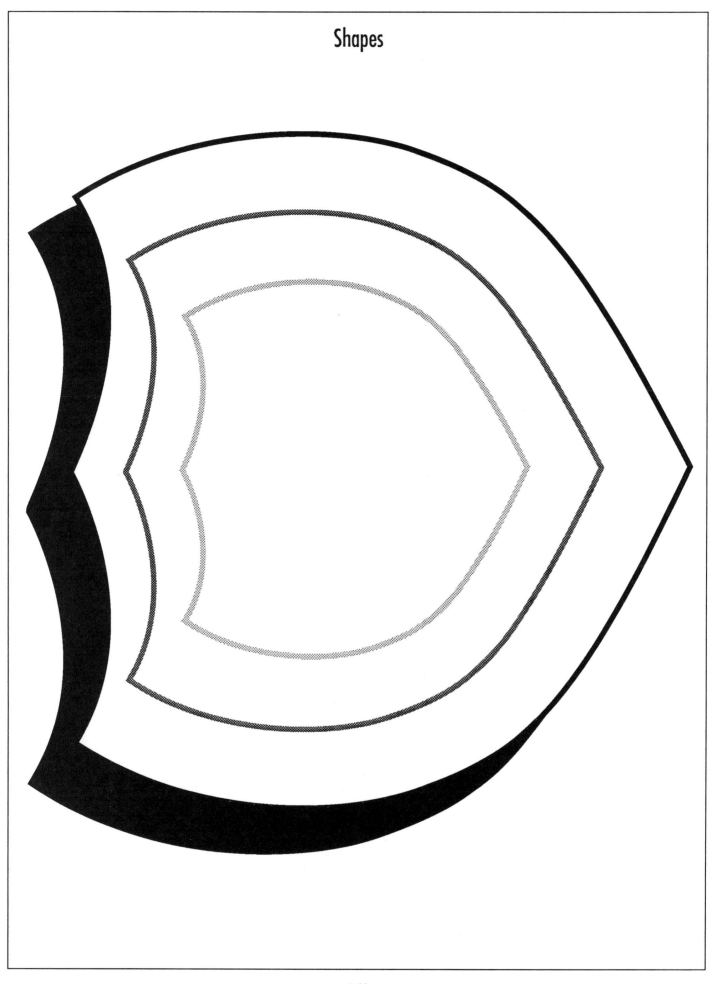

GA1341

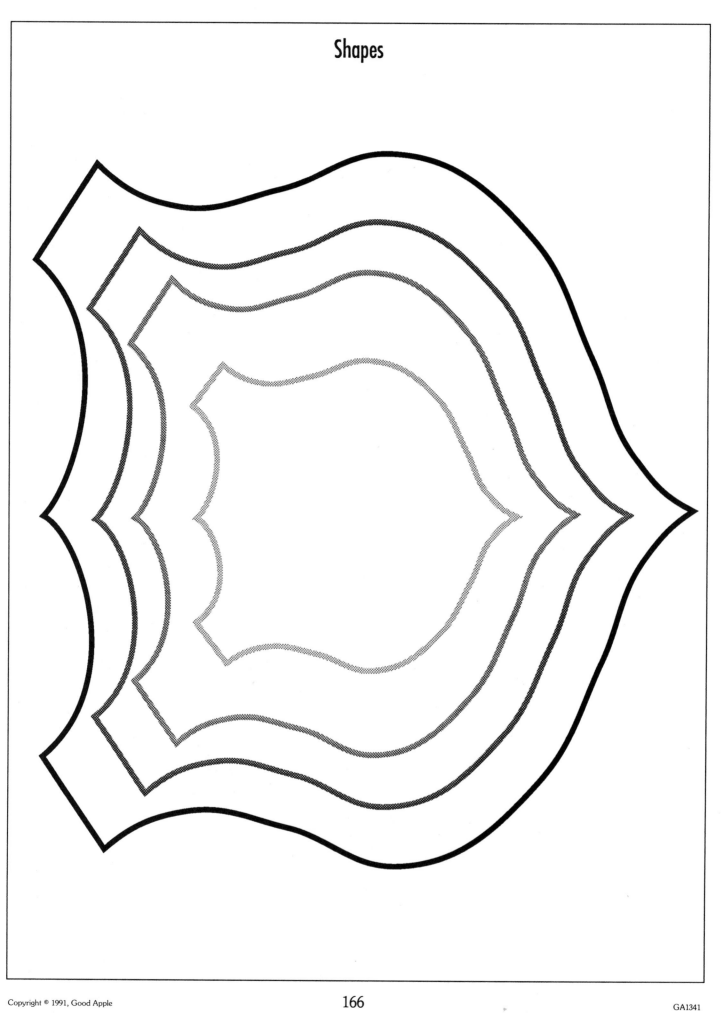

GA1341

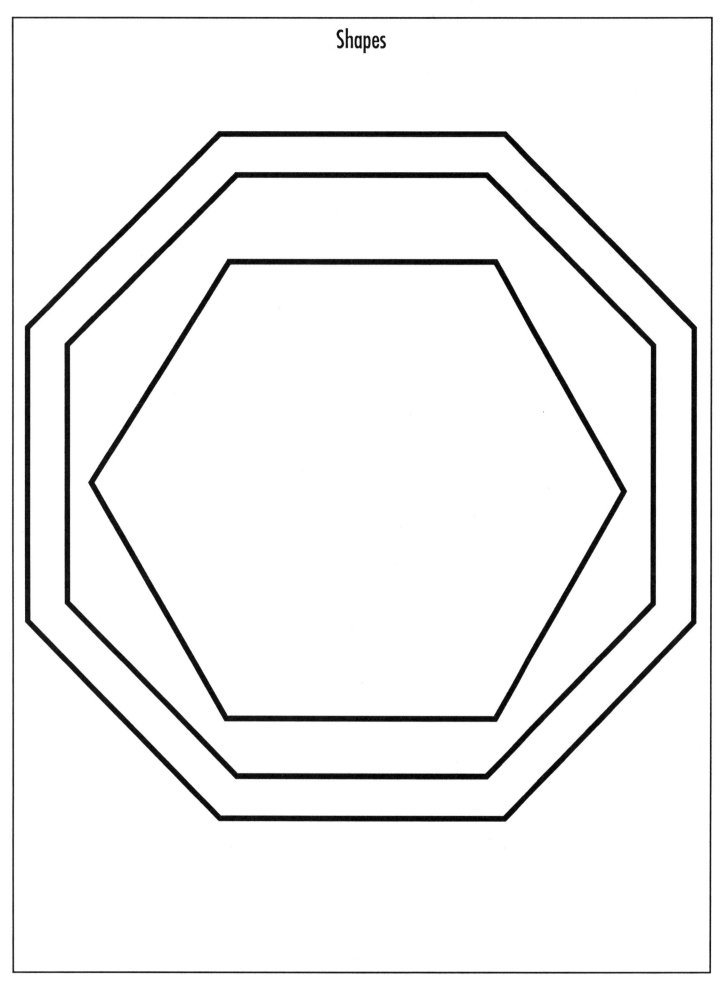

Shapes

168

GA1341

GA1341

Shapes

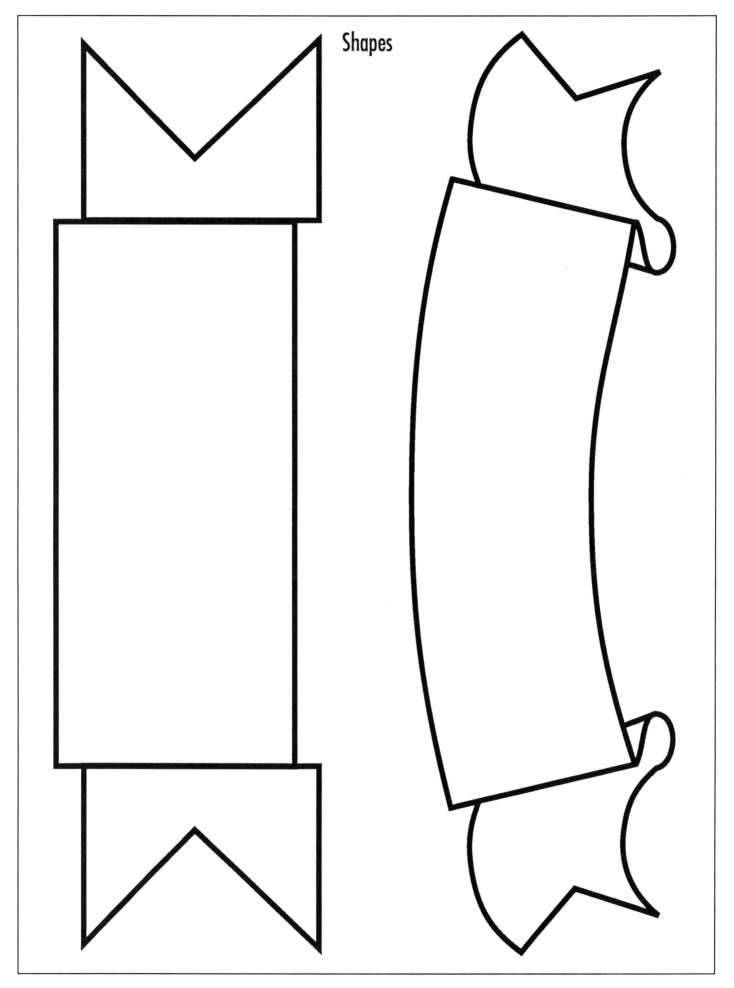

GA1341

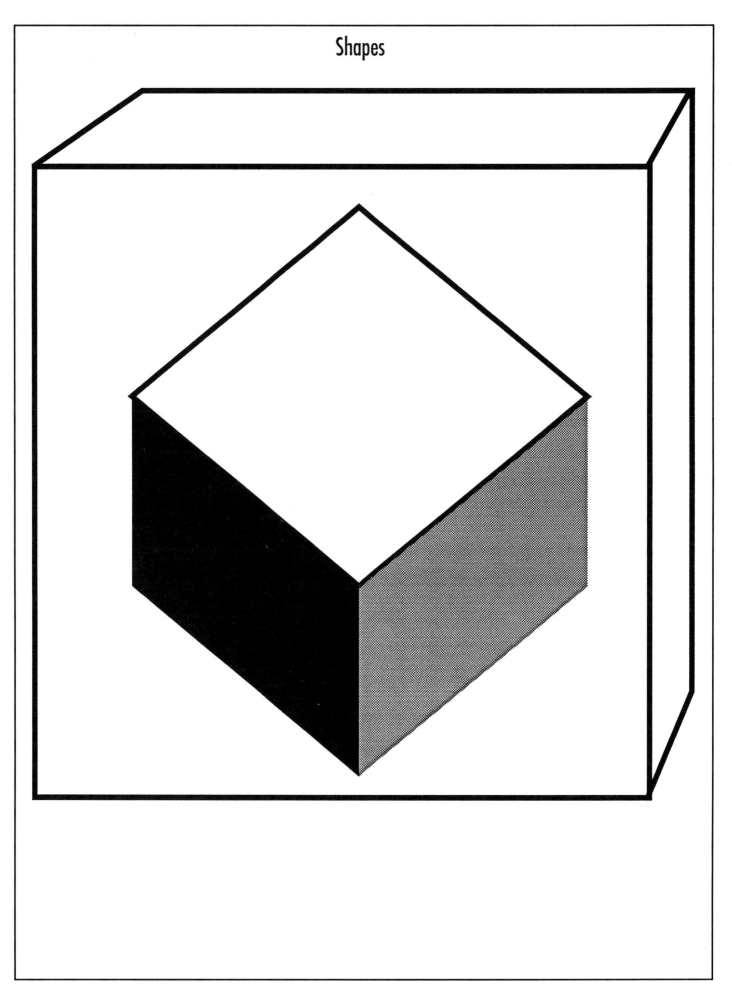

172

Shapes

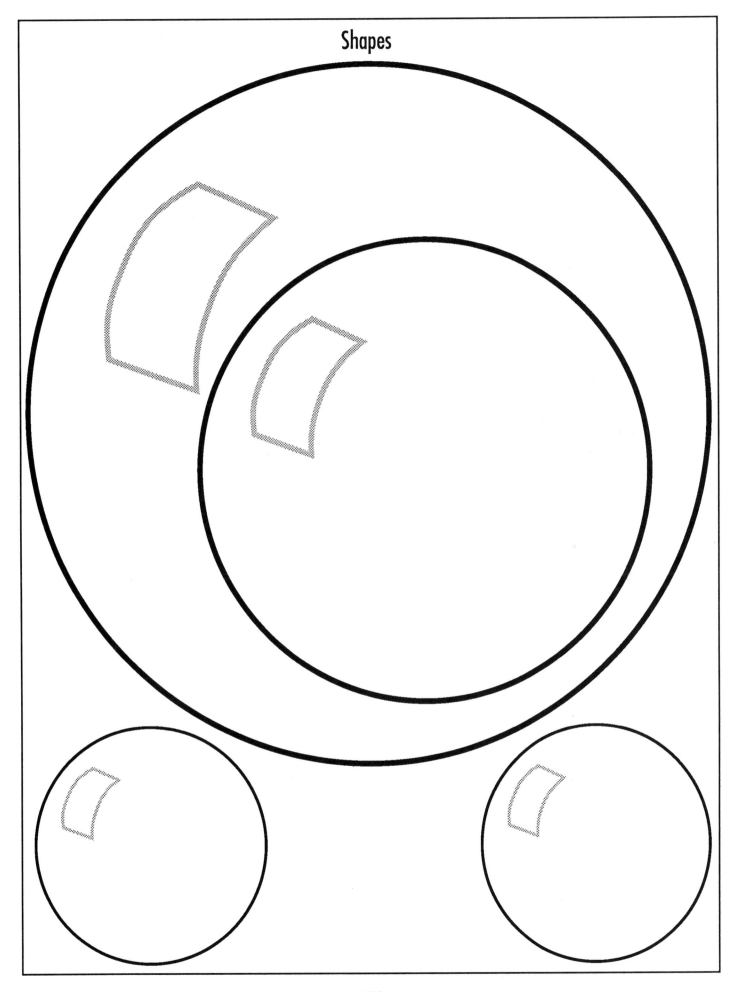

173

GA1341

GA1341

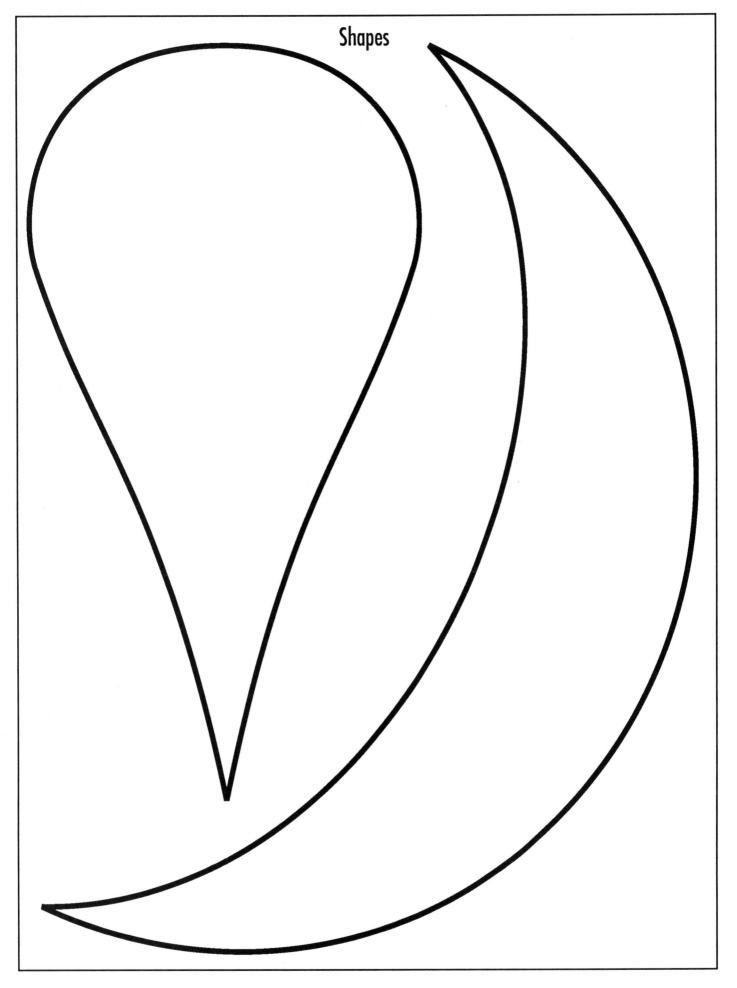

GA1341

Shapes

176

GA1341

GA1341

179

GA1341

Colors

GA1341

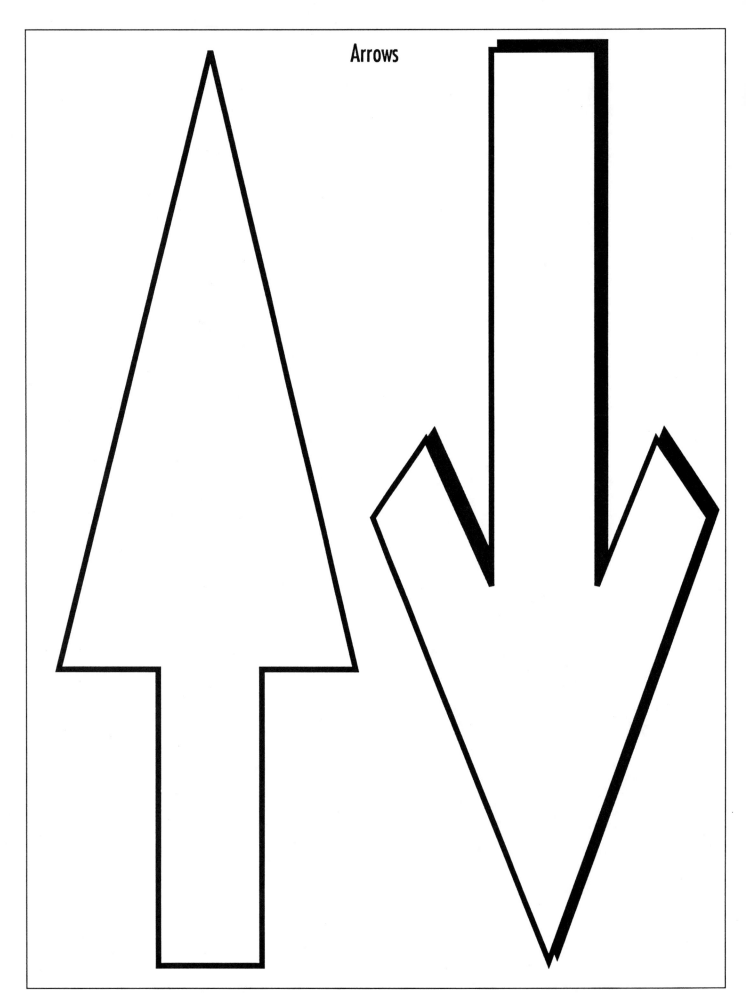

GA1341

185

GA1341

Arrows

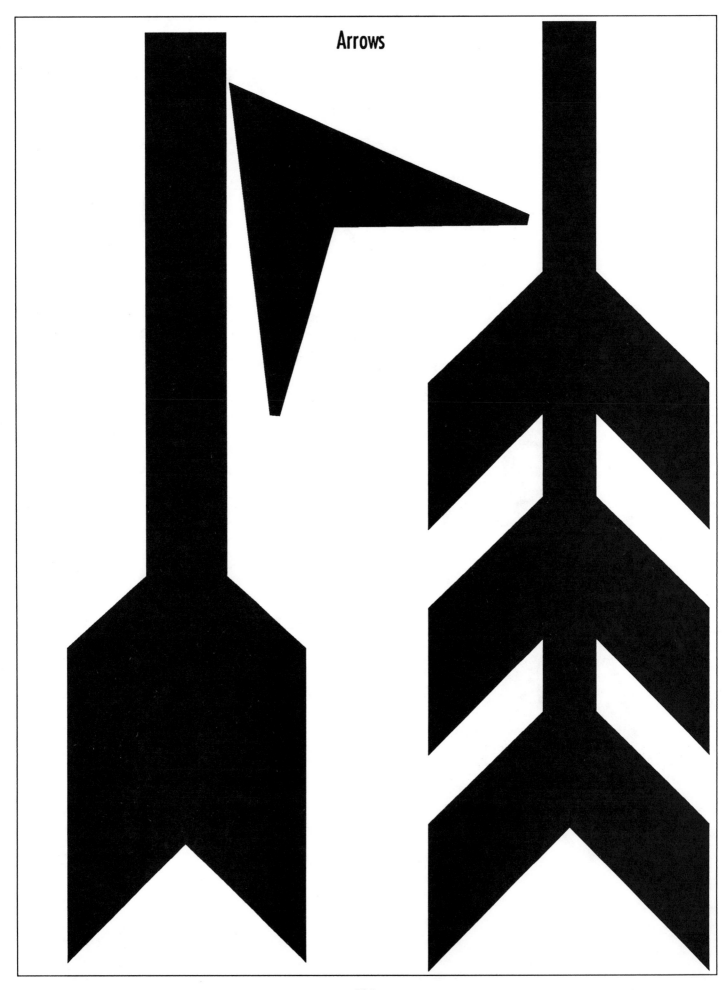

186

GA1341

187

GA1341

Mammals

GA1341

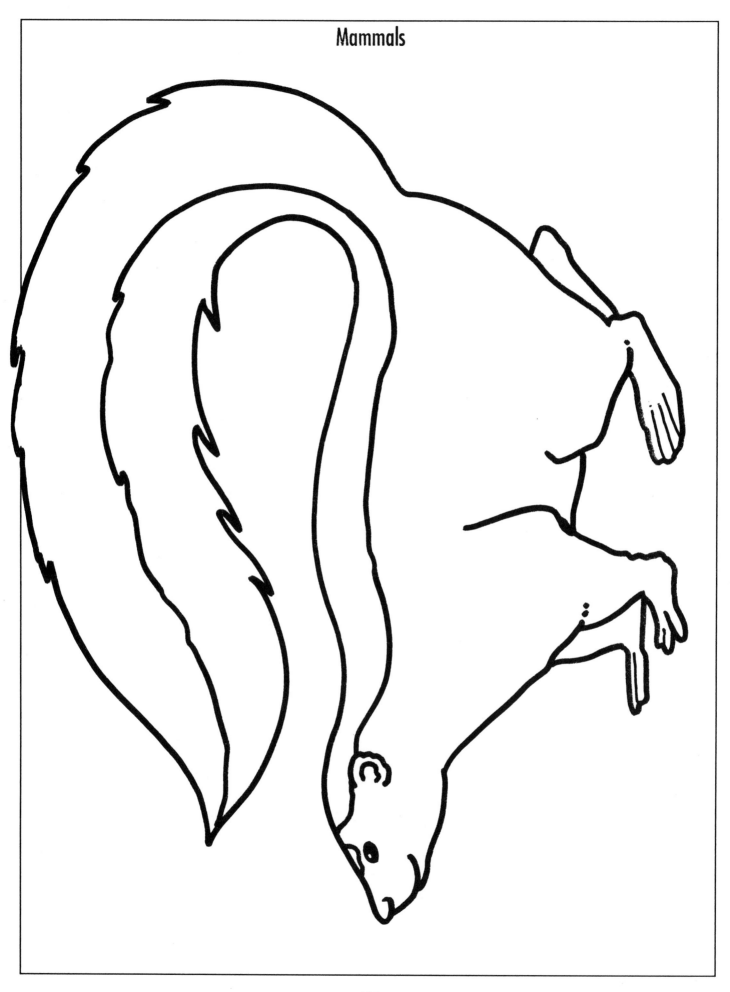

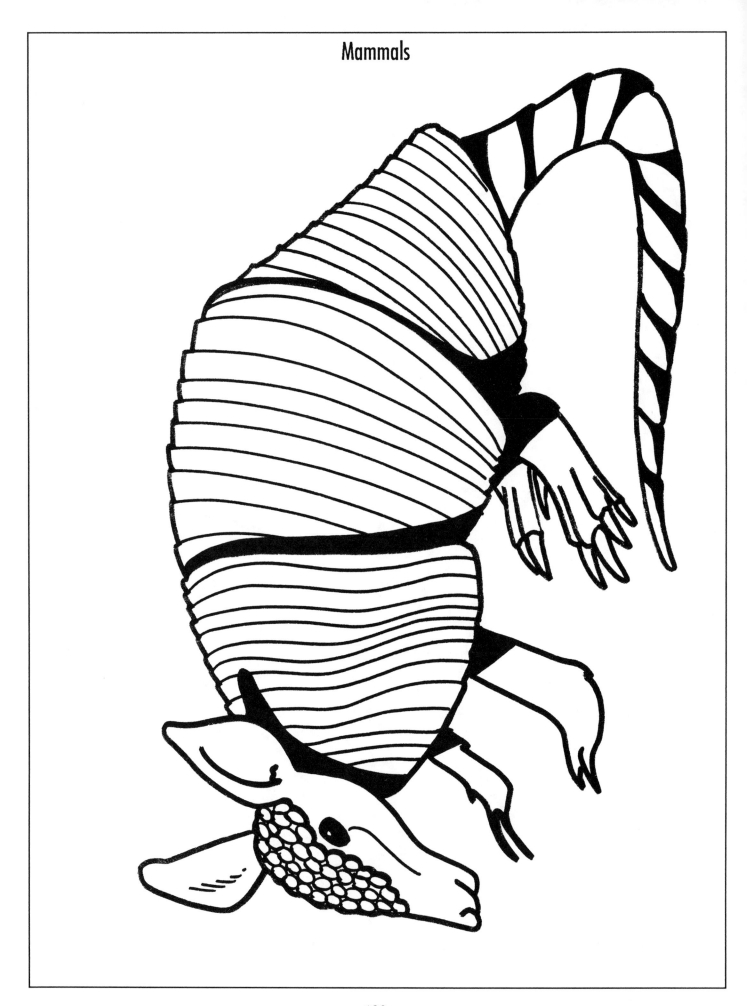

190

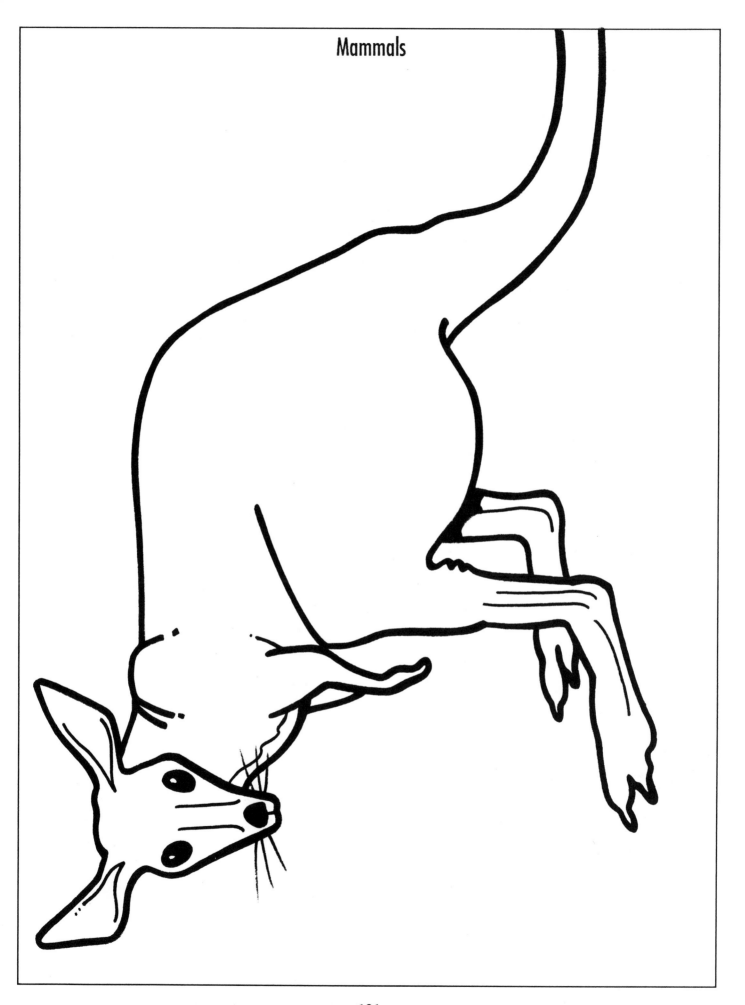

193

Mammals

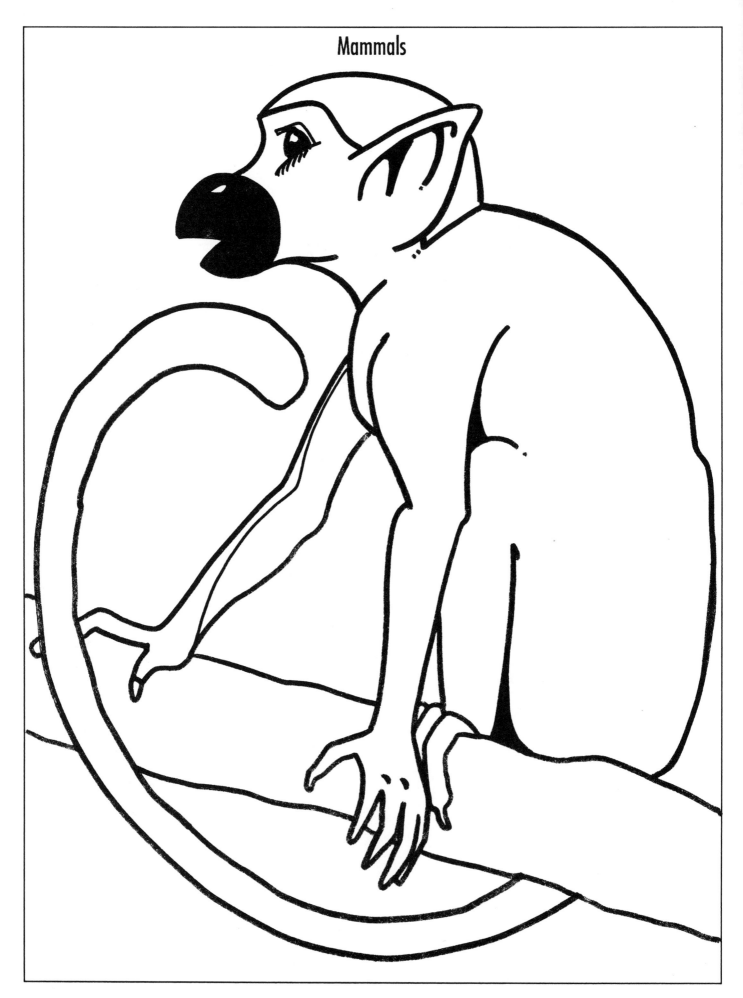

GA1341

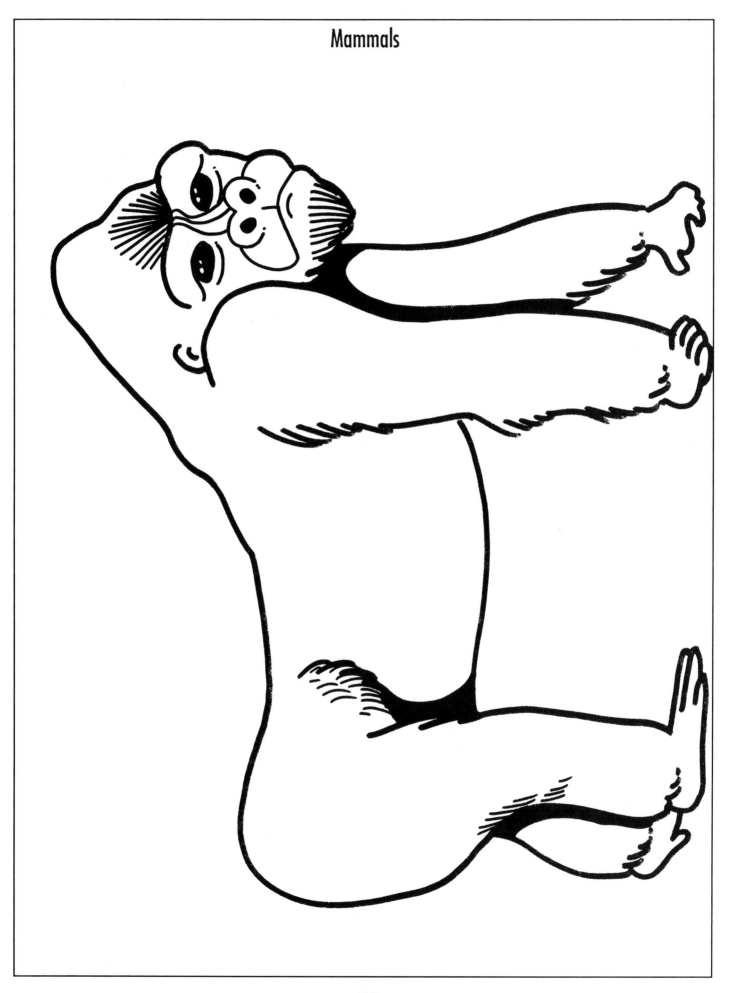

195

Mammals

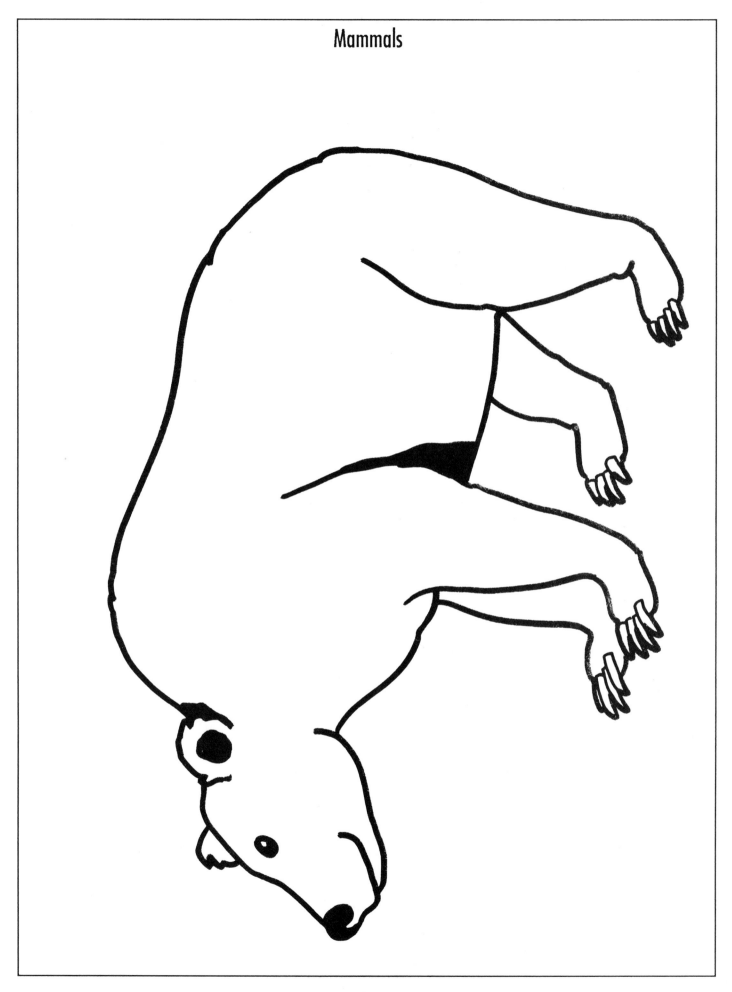

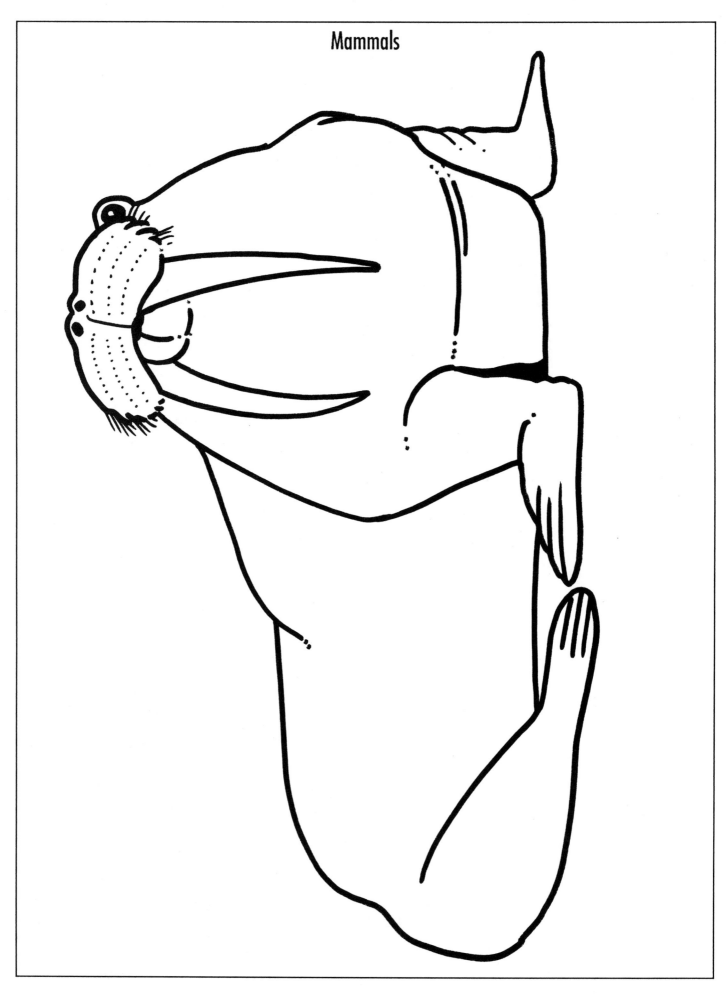

199

GA1341

Mammals

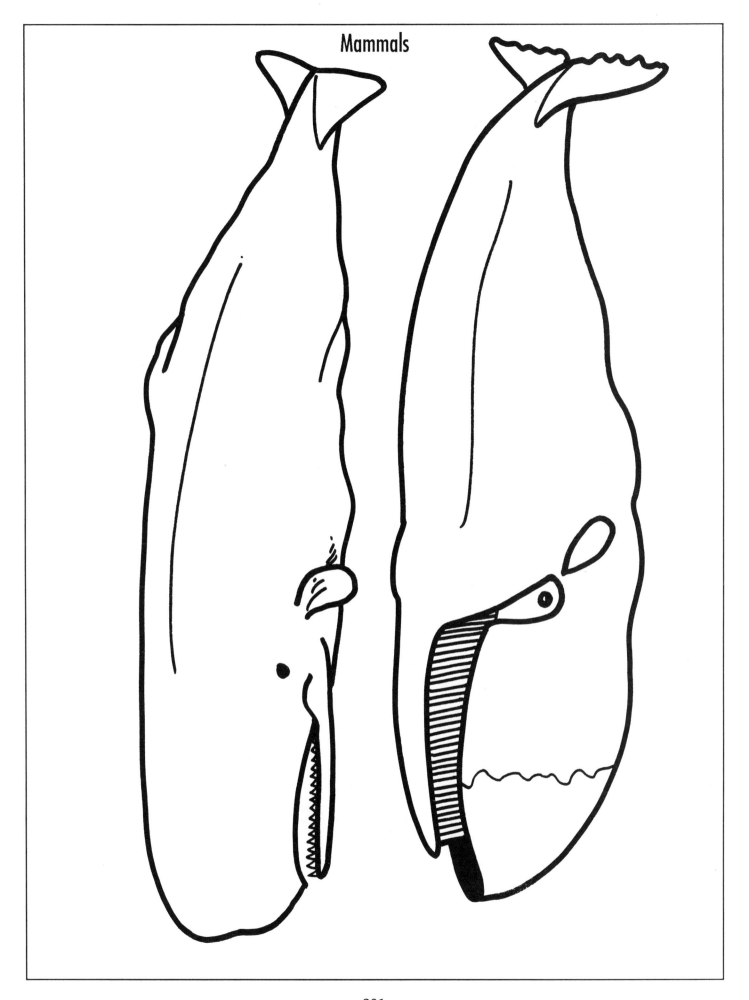

GA1341

Mammals

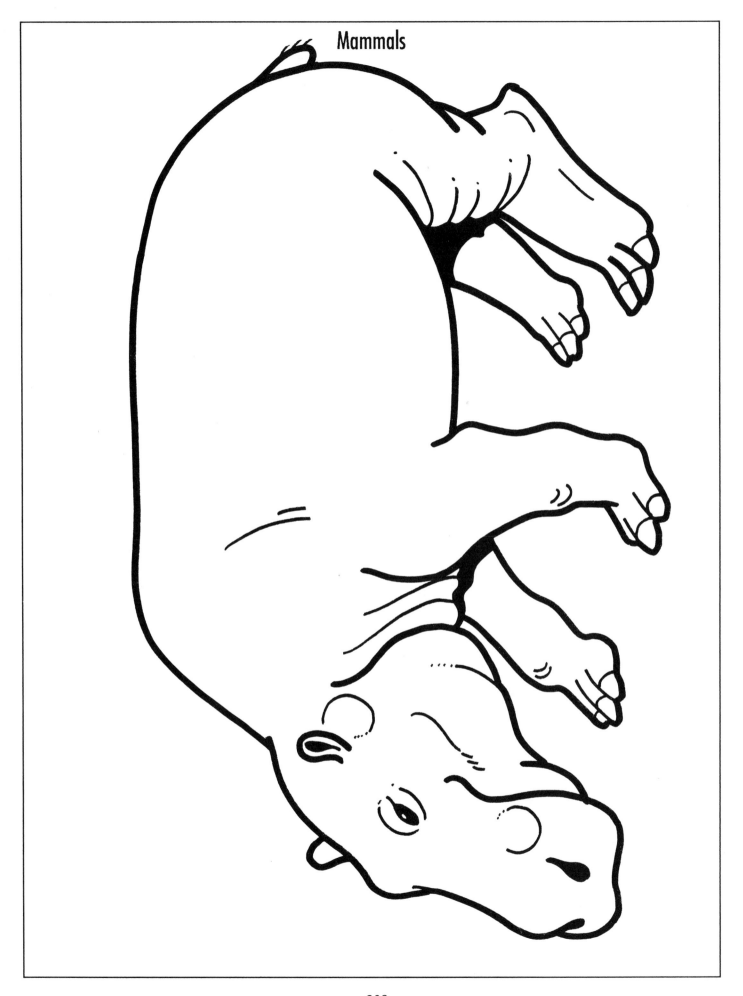

GA1341

GA1341

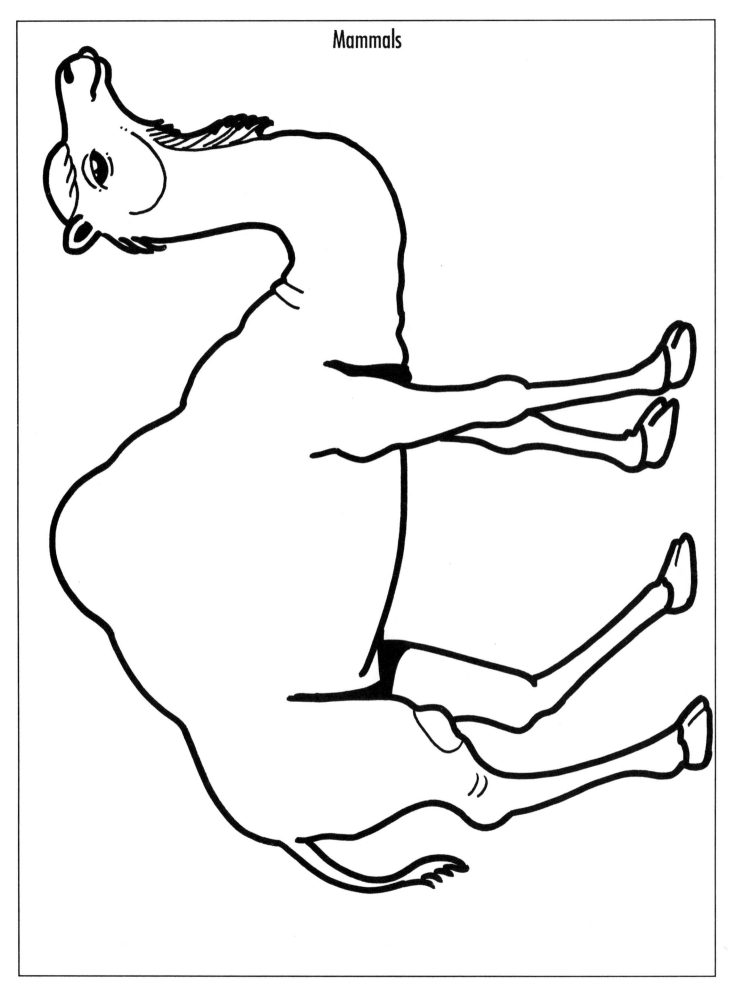

GA1341

GA1341

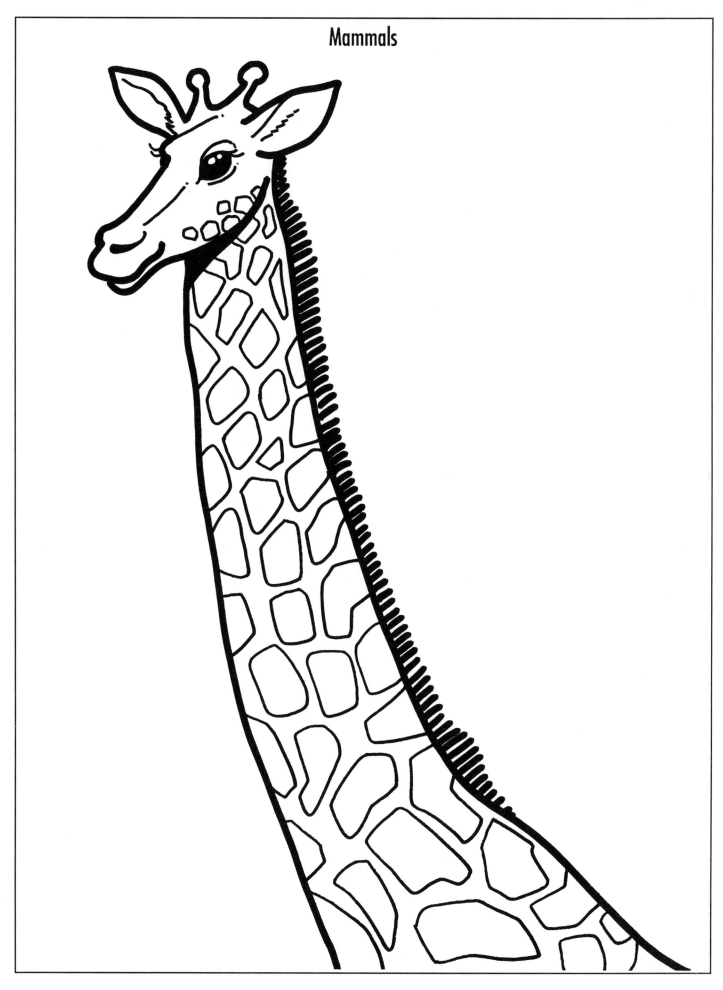

GA1341

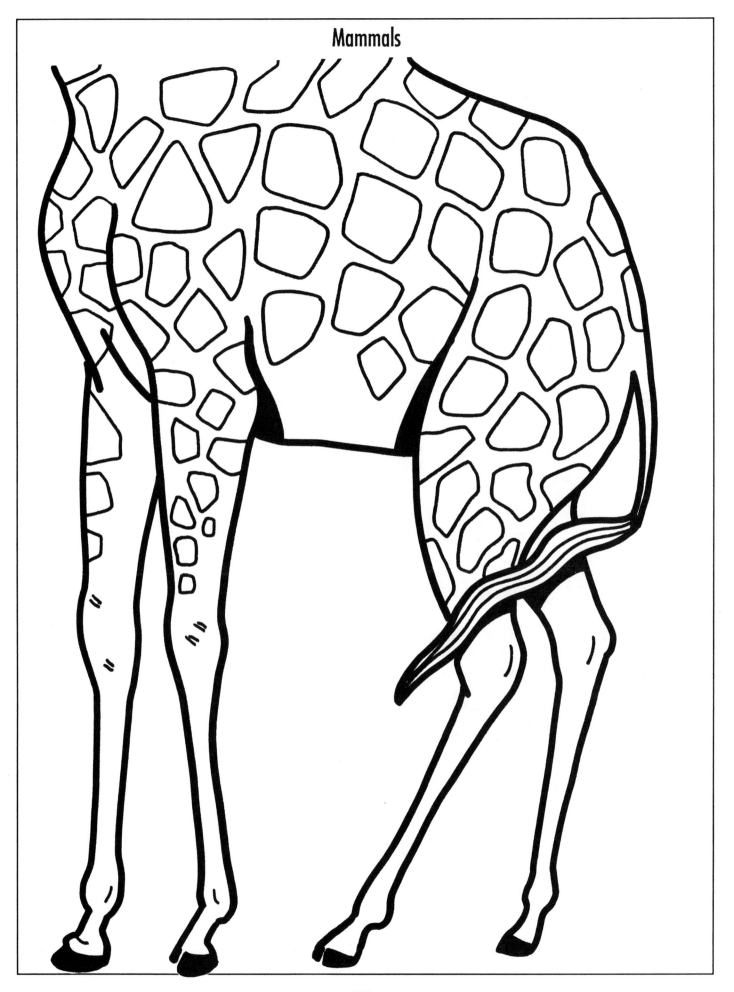

GA1341

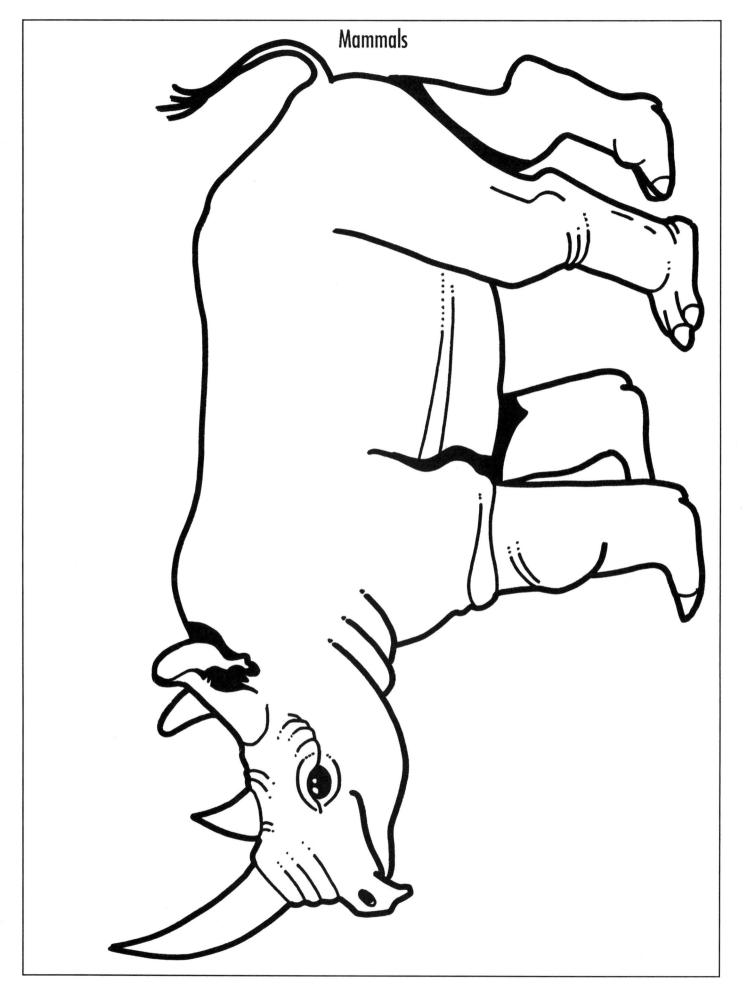

211

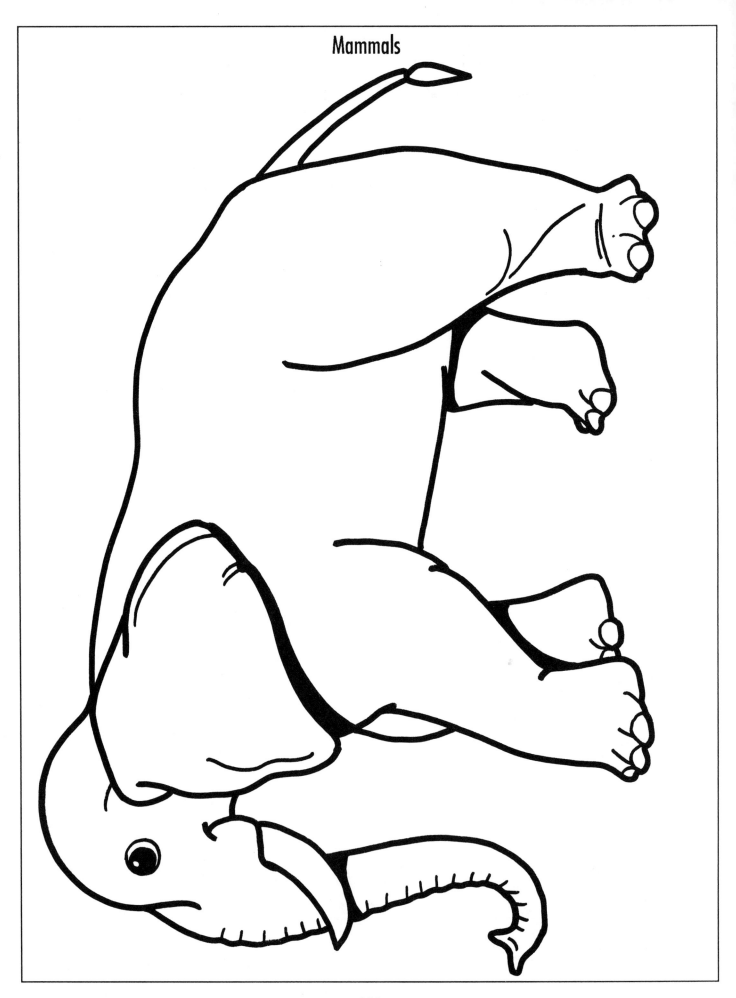

Mammals

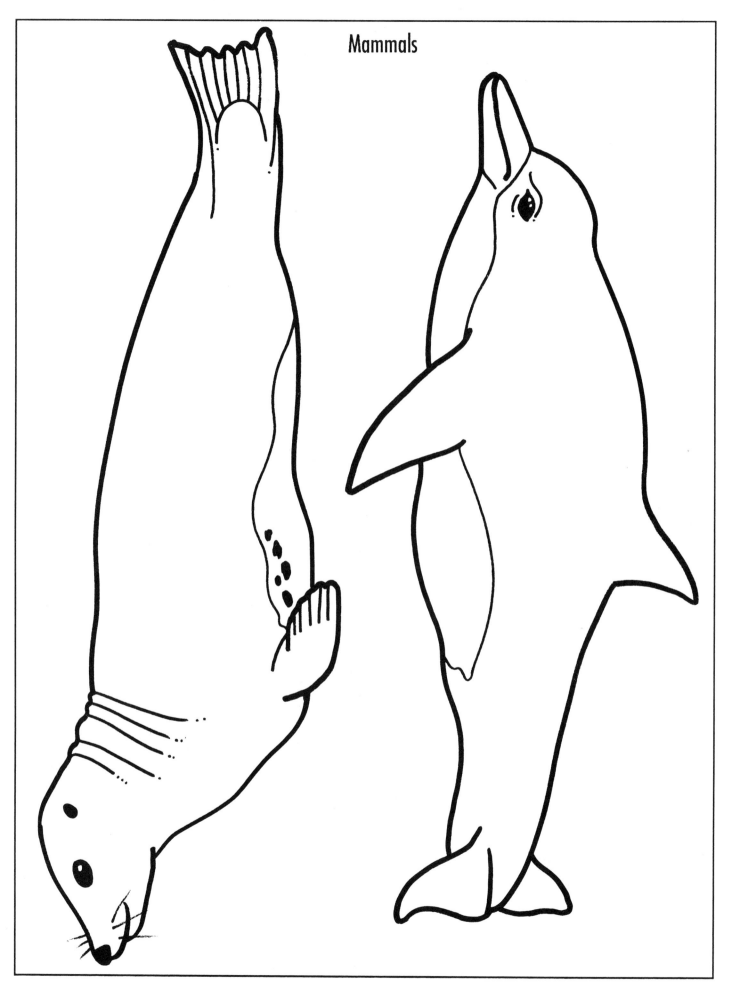

213

GA1341

Birds

214

GA1341

GA1341

219

Birds

Use peacock pattern by tracing the peacock's body first, centered on paper that is at least fifteen inches wide. Then trace the right and left side of the feathers behind the peacock. **OR** trace the body on one piece of paper and the plumage on another and glue the body on top of the plumage.

220

GA1341

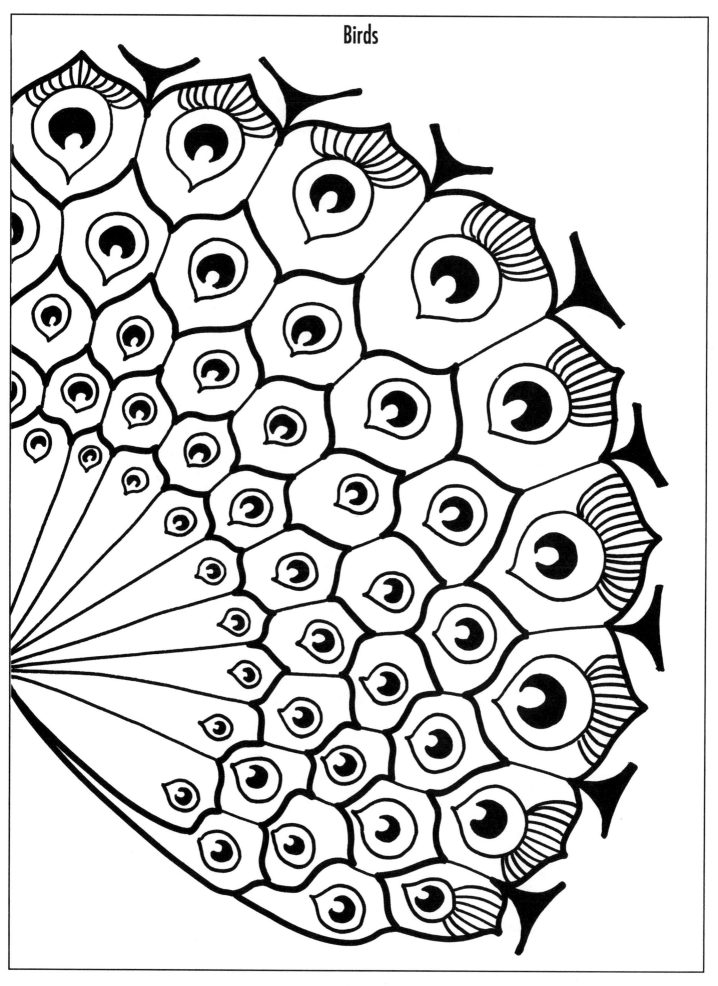

221

GA1341

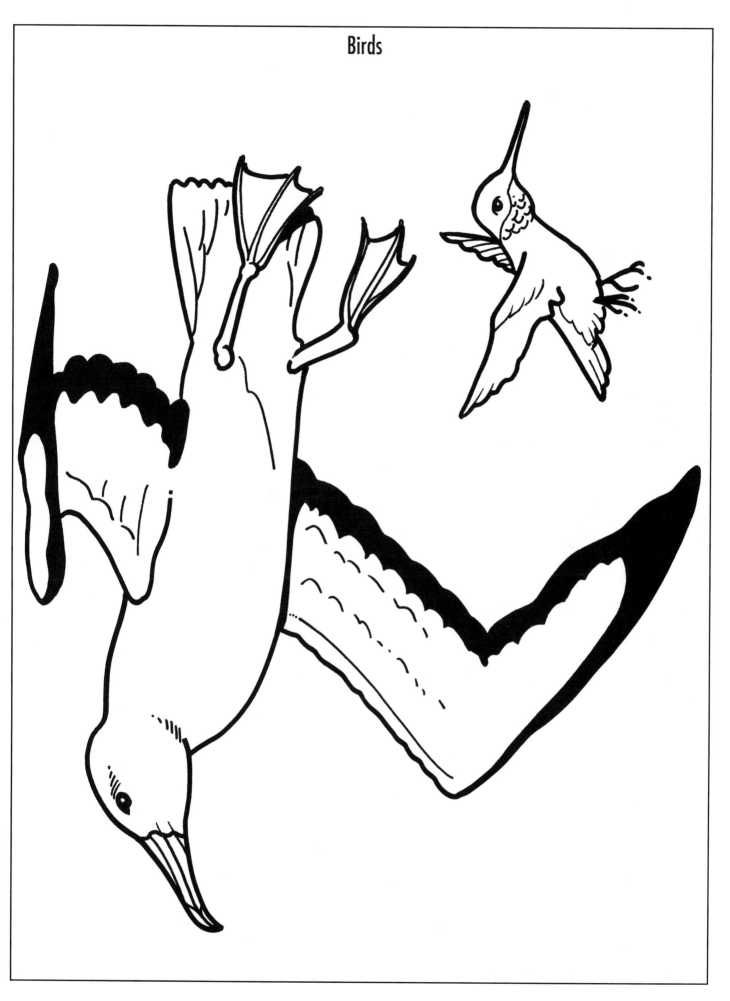

223

Birds

224

GA1341

GA1341

GA1341

GA1341

228

229

GA1341

Crustaceans

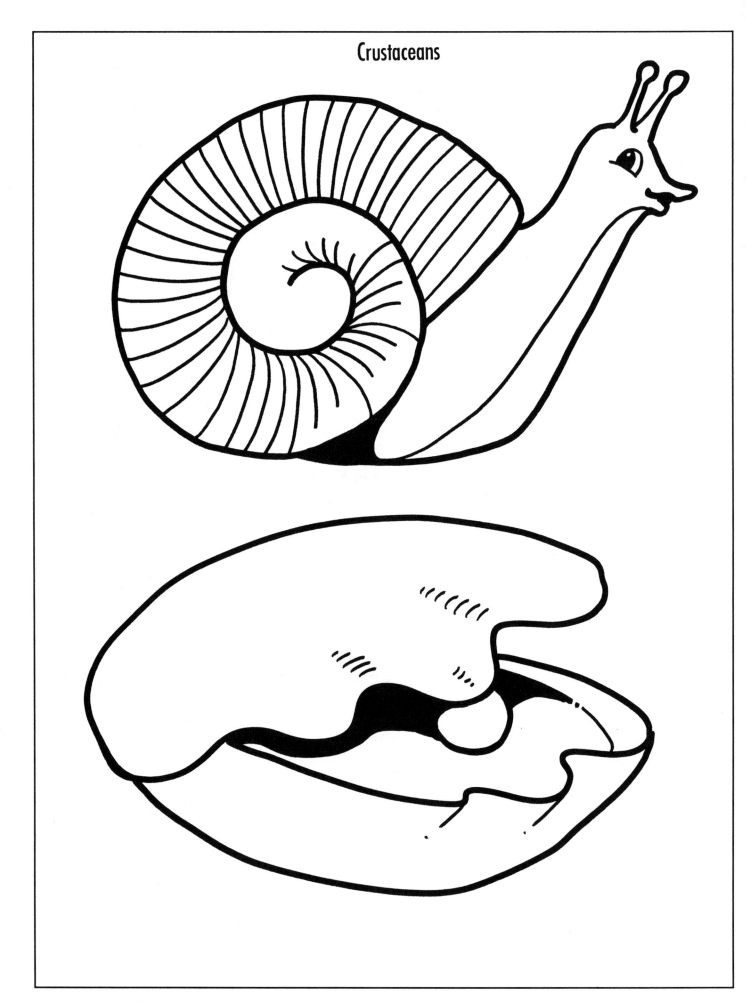

230

GA1341

Fish

Goldfish

Atlantic Flying Fish

231

GA1341

Fish

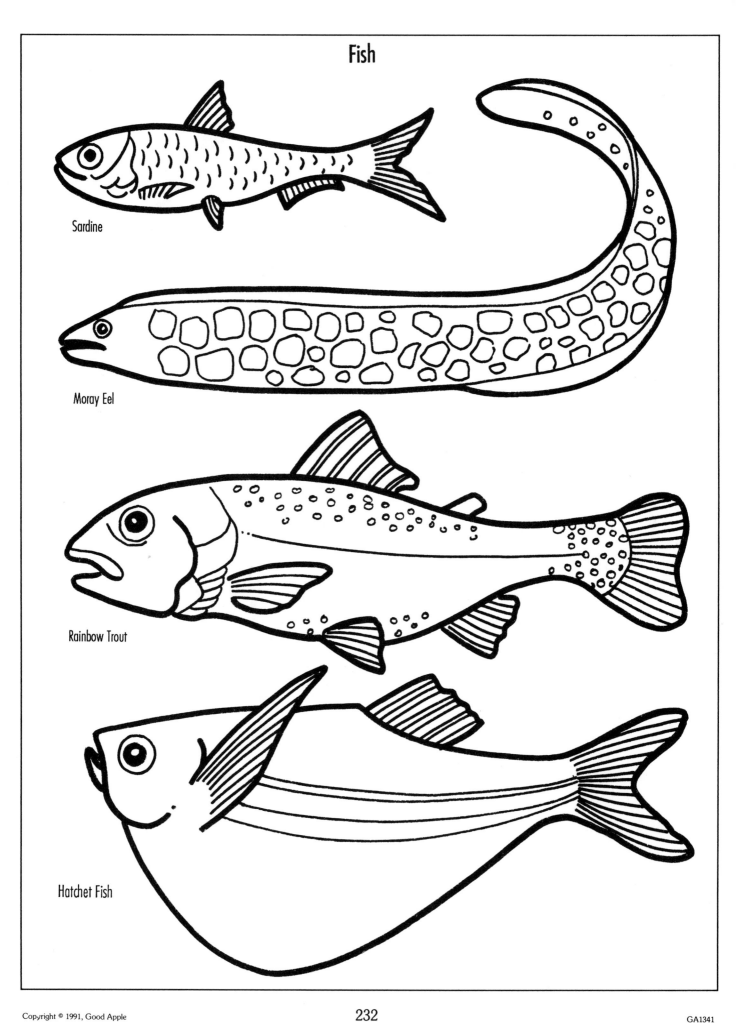

Sardine

Moray Eel

Rainbow Trout

Hatchet Fish

Fish

Shark

Monkfish

233

GA1341

Fish

Fish

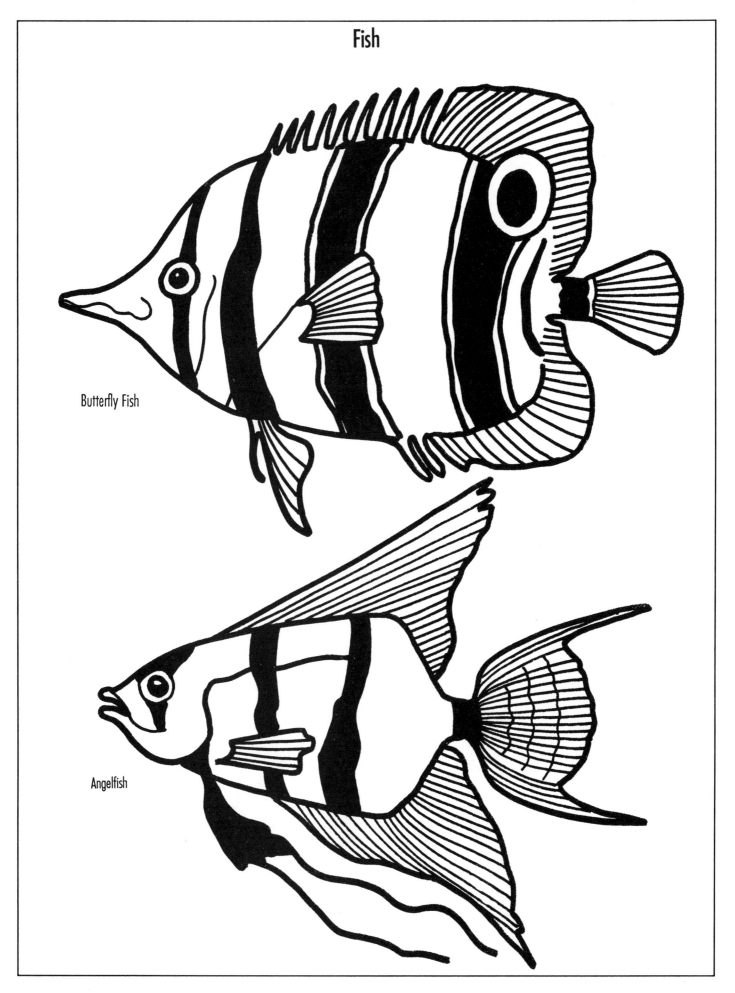

Butterfly Fish

Angelfish

235

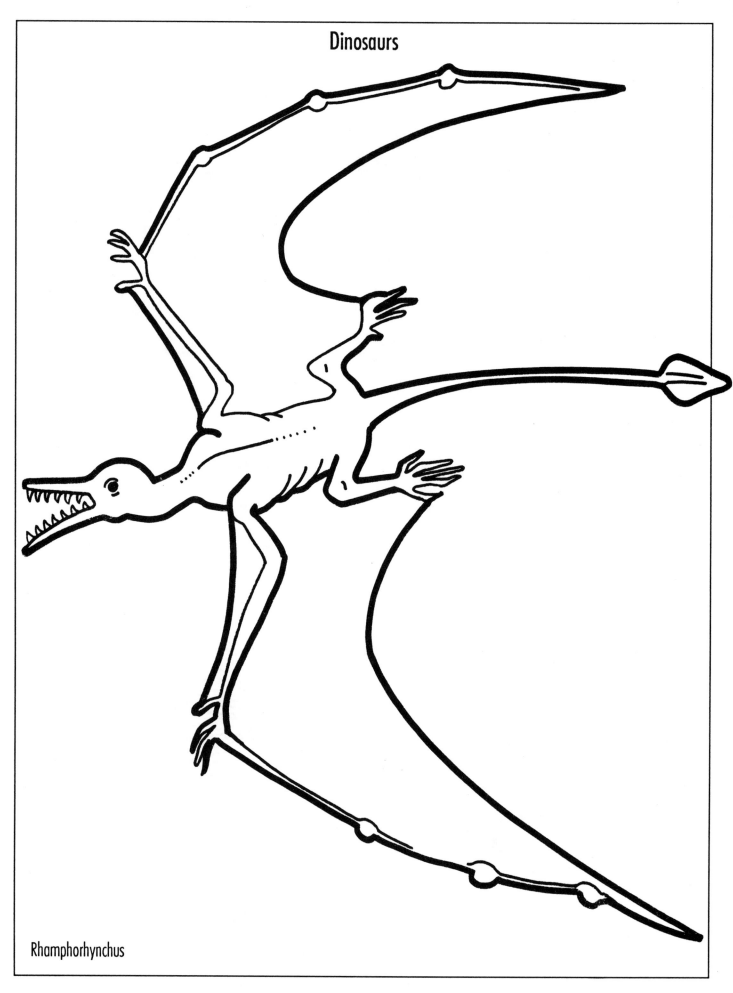

Rhamphorhynchus

Pteranodon

GA1341

Dimetrodon

GA1341

Iguanodon

GA1341

Dinosaurs

Brachiosaurus

240

Anatosaurus

GA1341

Dinosaurs

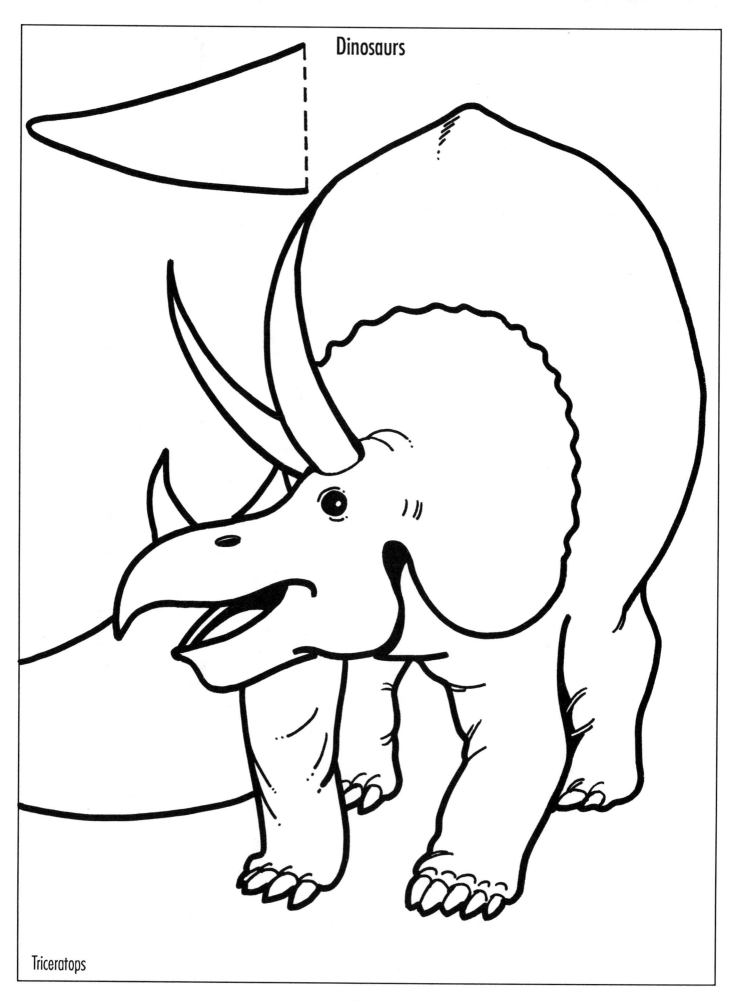

Triceratops

242

GA1341

Stegosaurus

GA1341

Elasmosaurus

GA1341

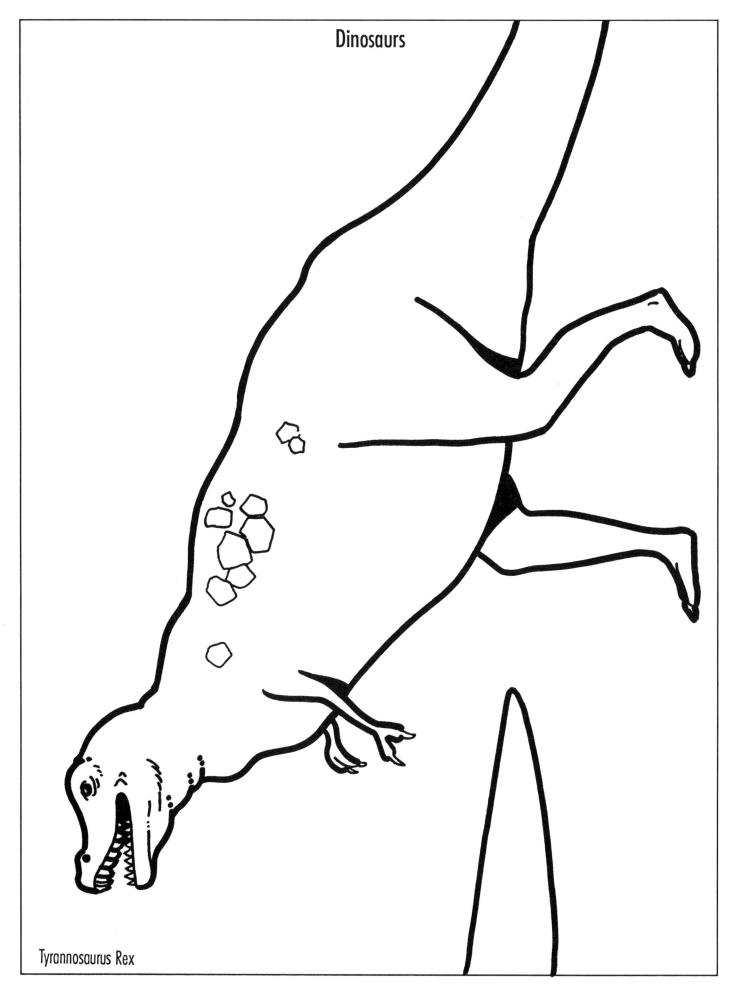

Tyrannosaurus Rex

GA1341

Parasaurolophus

GA1341

GA1341

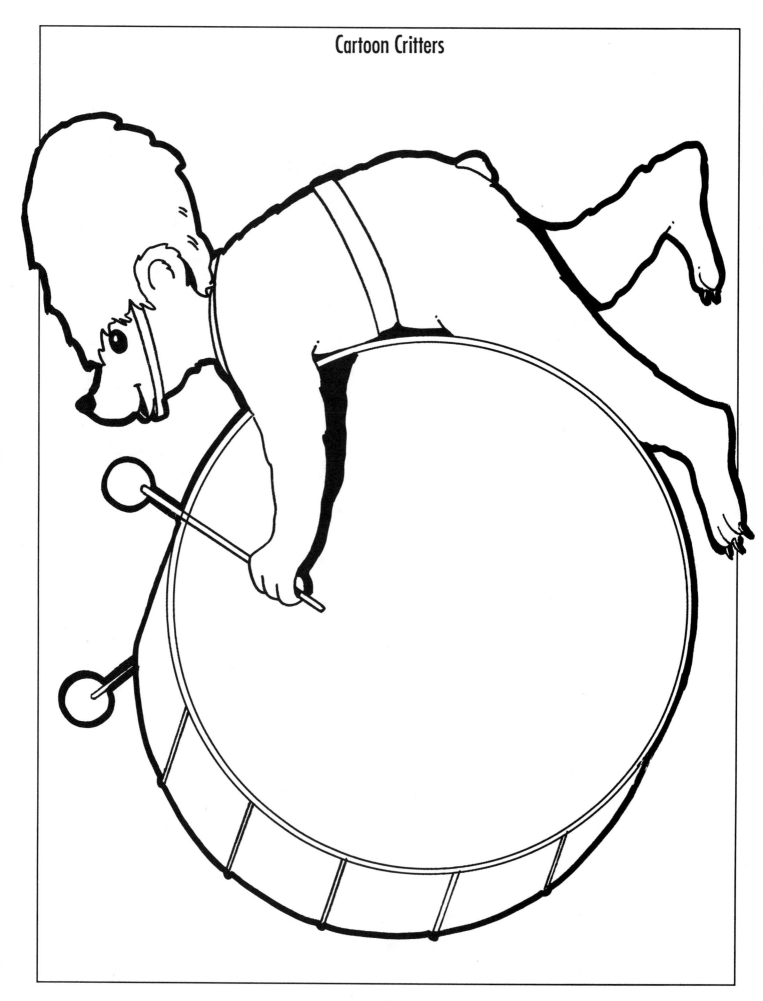

249

GA1341

GA1341

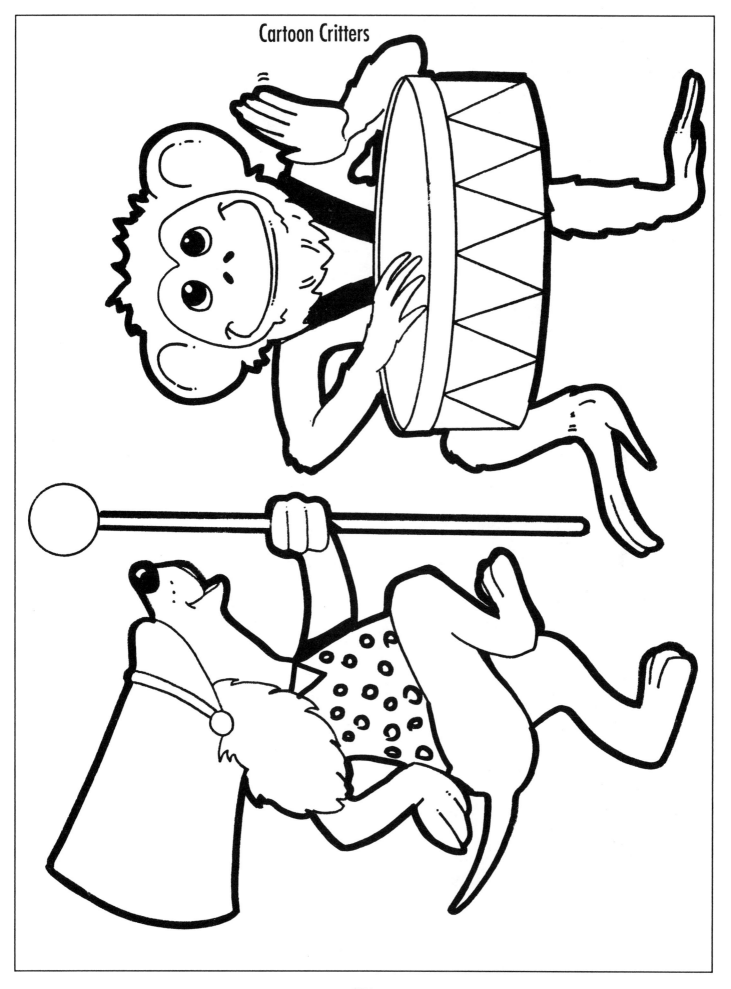

251

GA1341

253

GA1341

254

GA1341

GA1341

256

GA1341

Children

Children

258

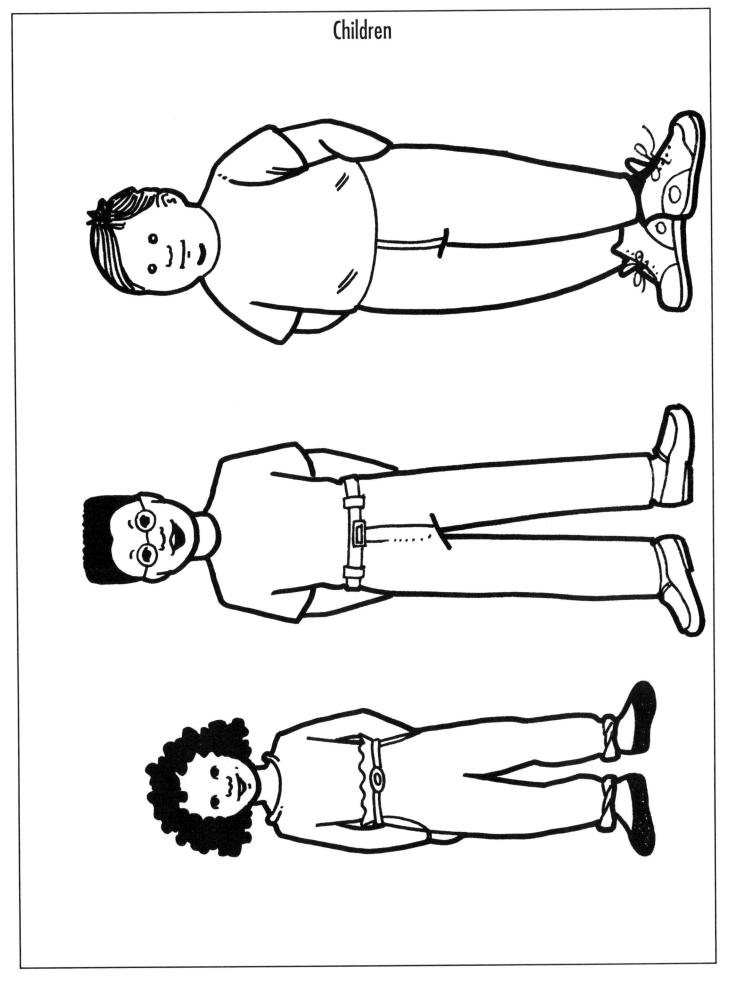

259

Children

260

GA1341

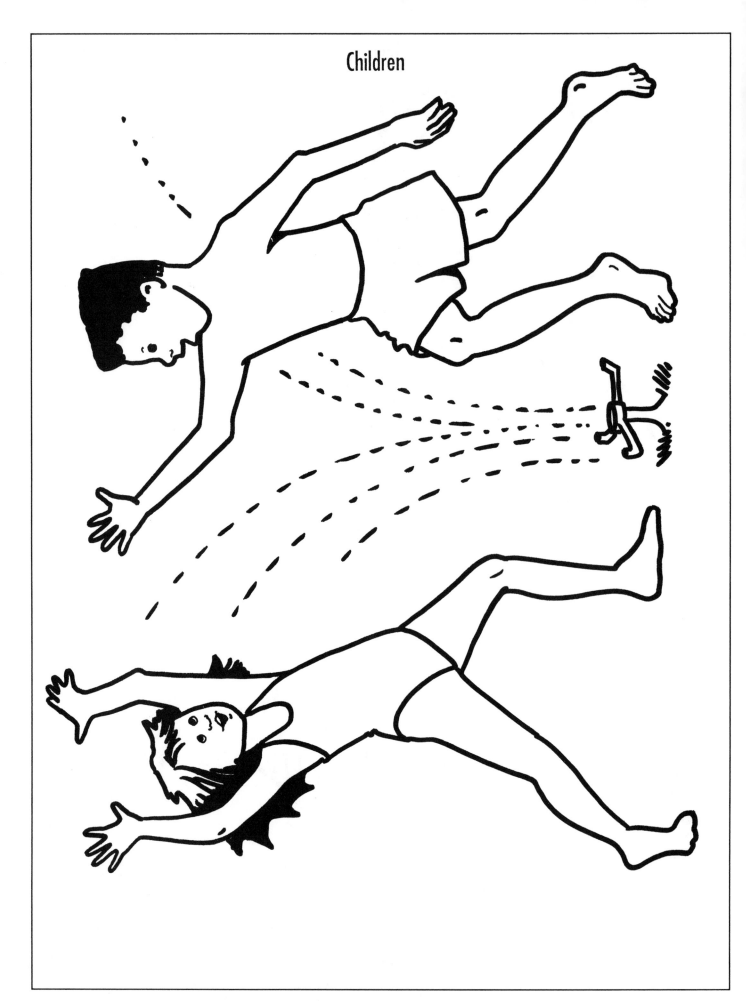

GA1341

GA1341

GA1341

268

GA1341

GA1341

271

272

GA1341

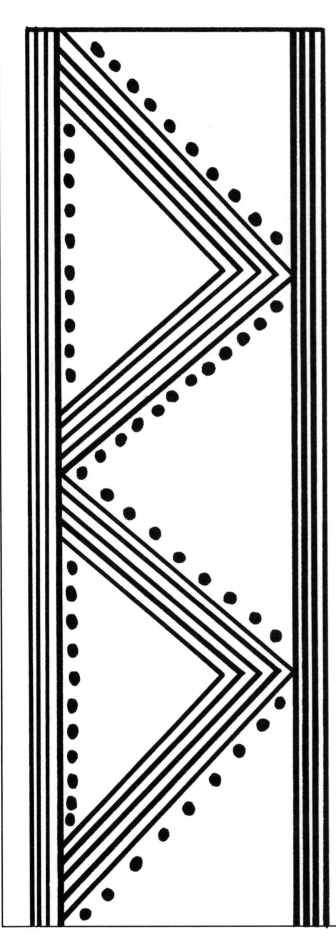

GA1341

GA1341

GA1341

GA1341

277

GA1341

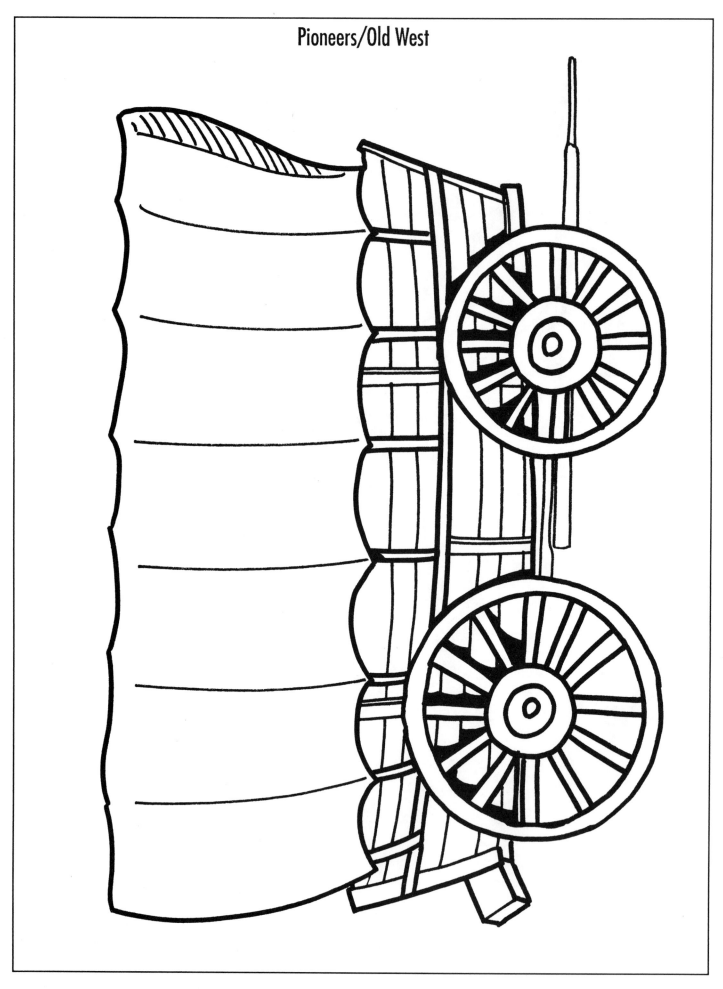

278

GA1341

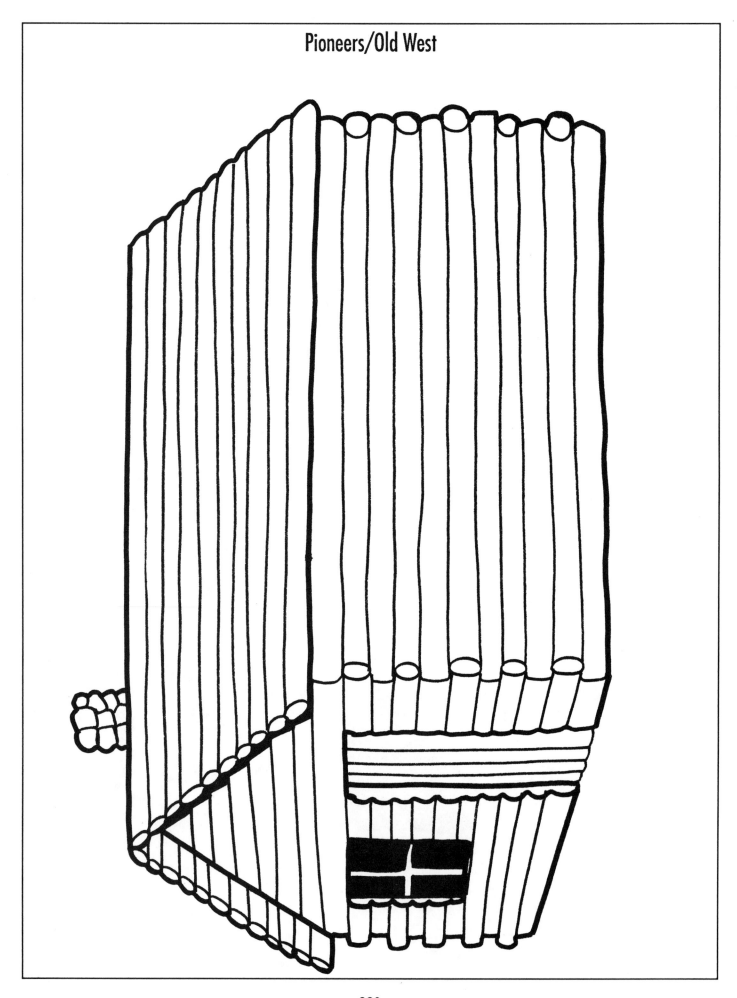

280

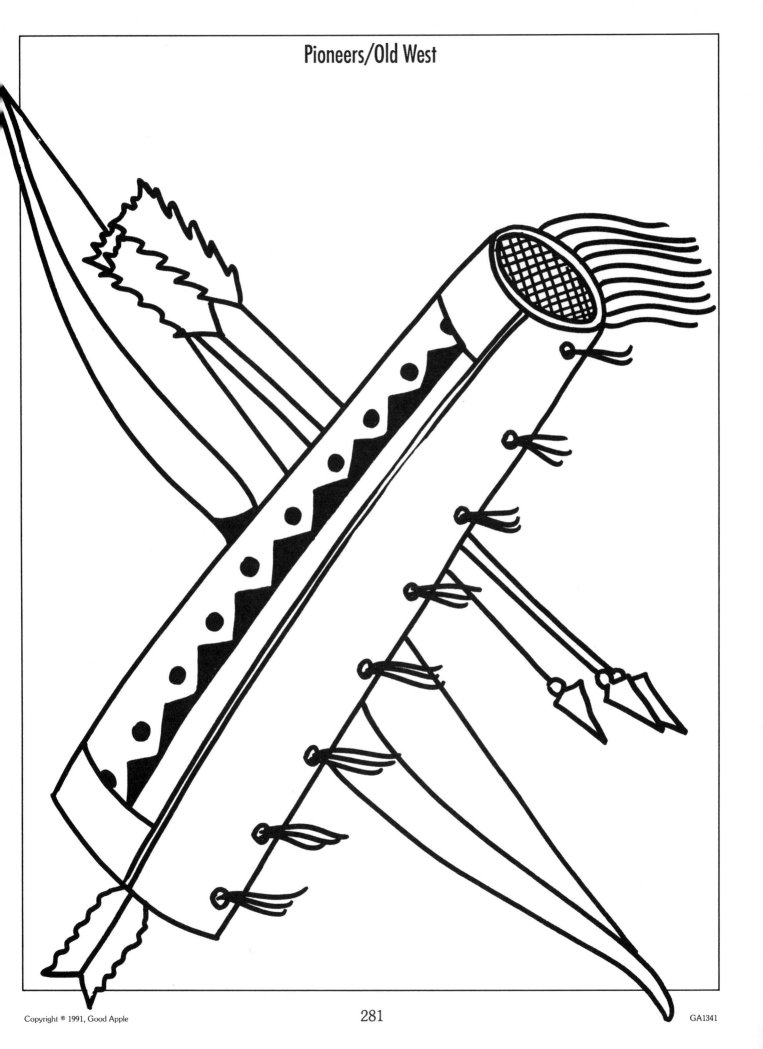

GA1341

Patriotic

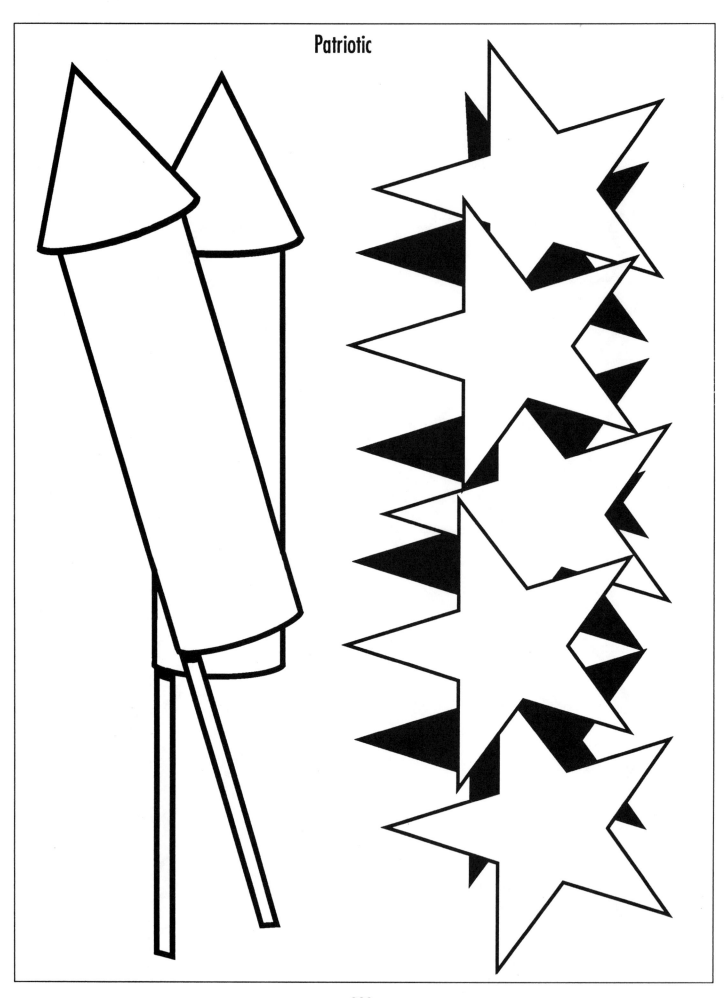

282

Patriotic

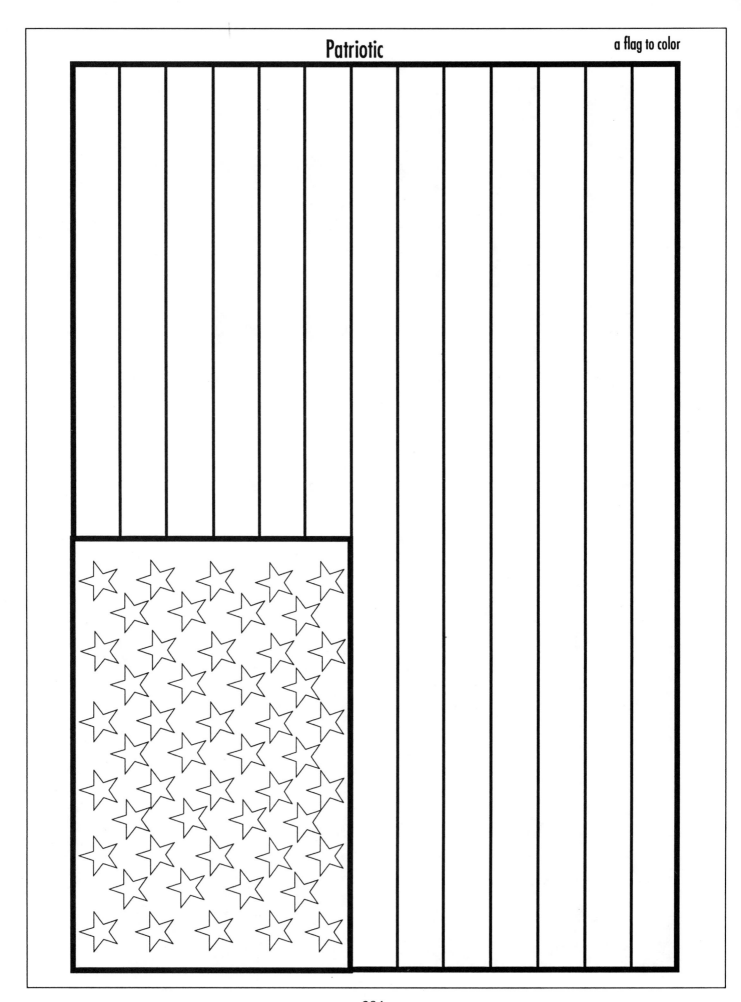

GA1341

GA1341

Patriotic

286

GA1341

GA1341

GA1341

GA1341

Peace

Peace

291

GA1341

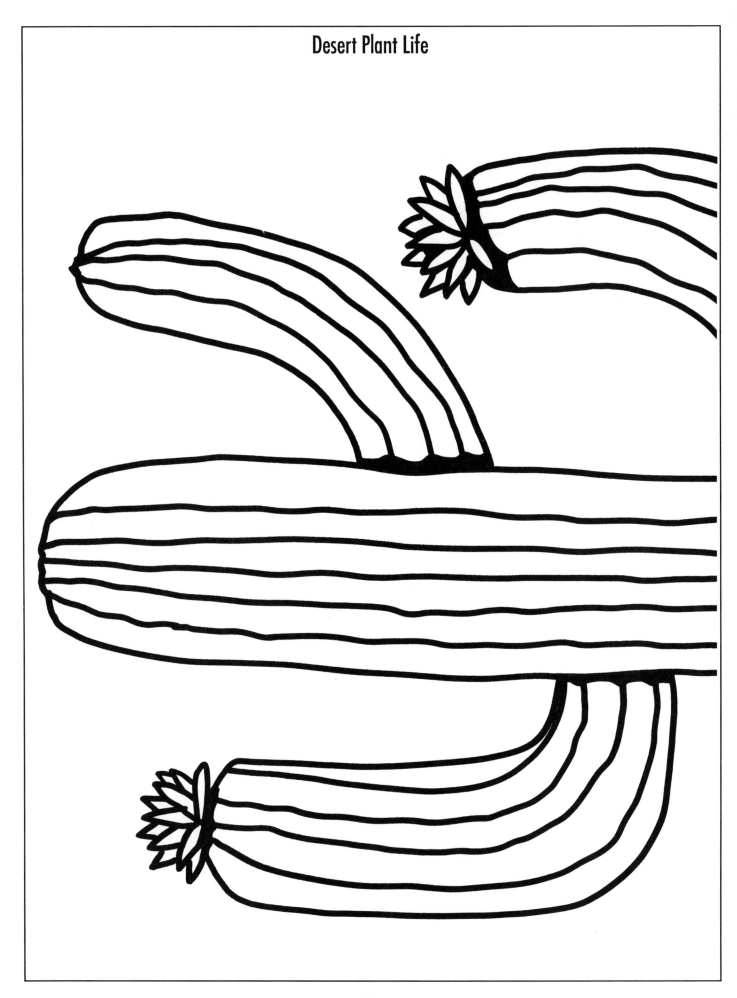

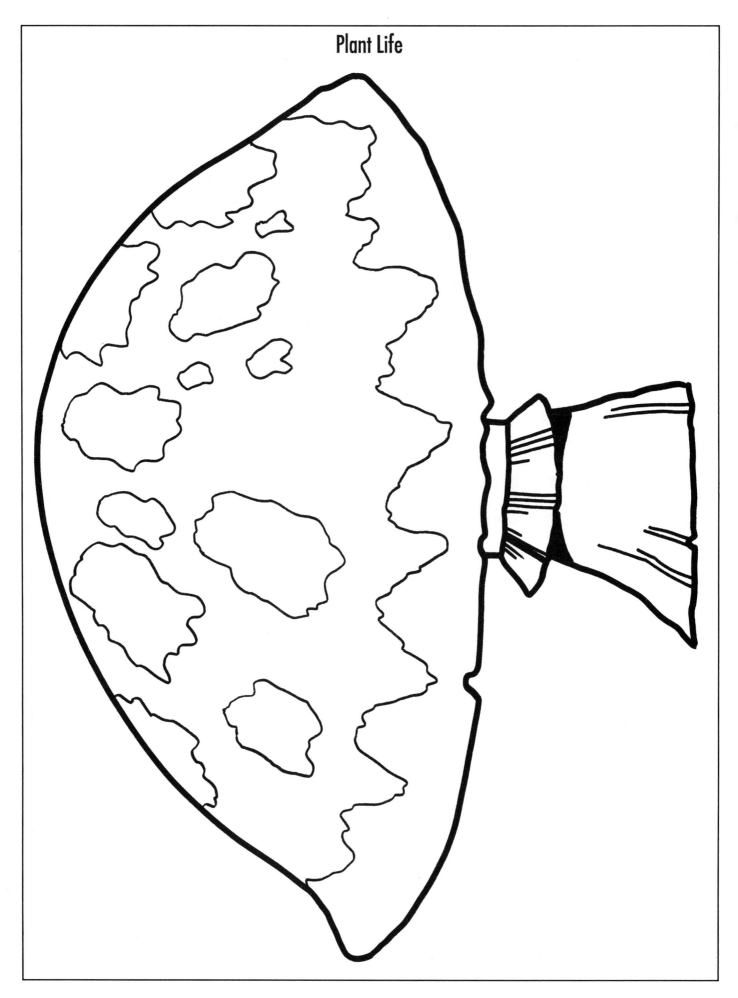

GA1341

297

GA1341

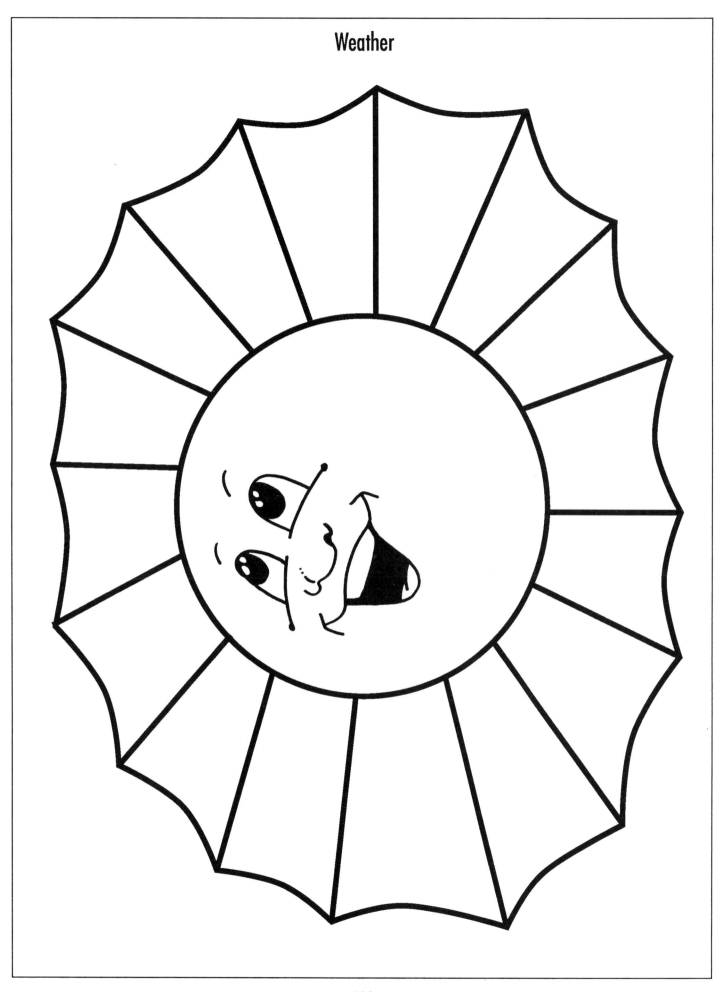

299

Weather

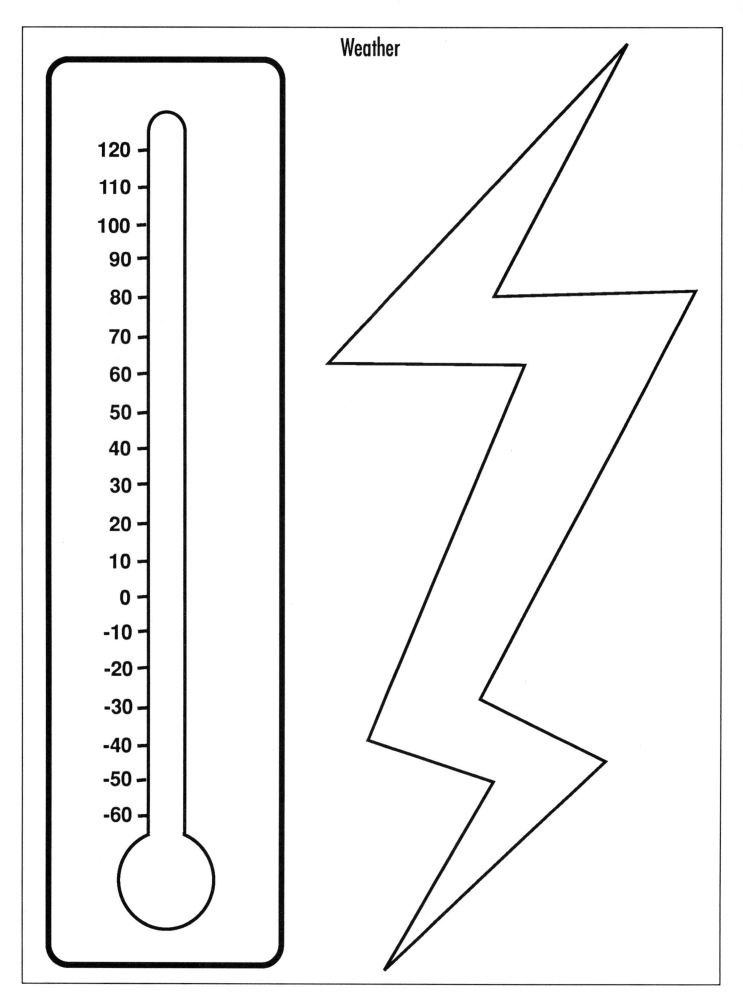

300

GA1341

GA1341

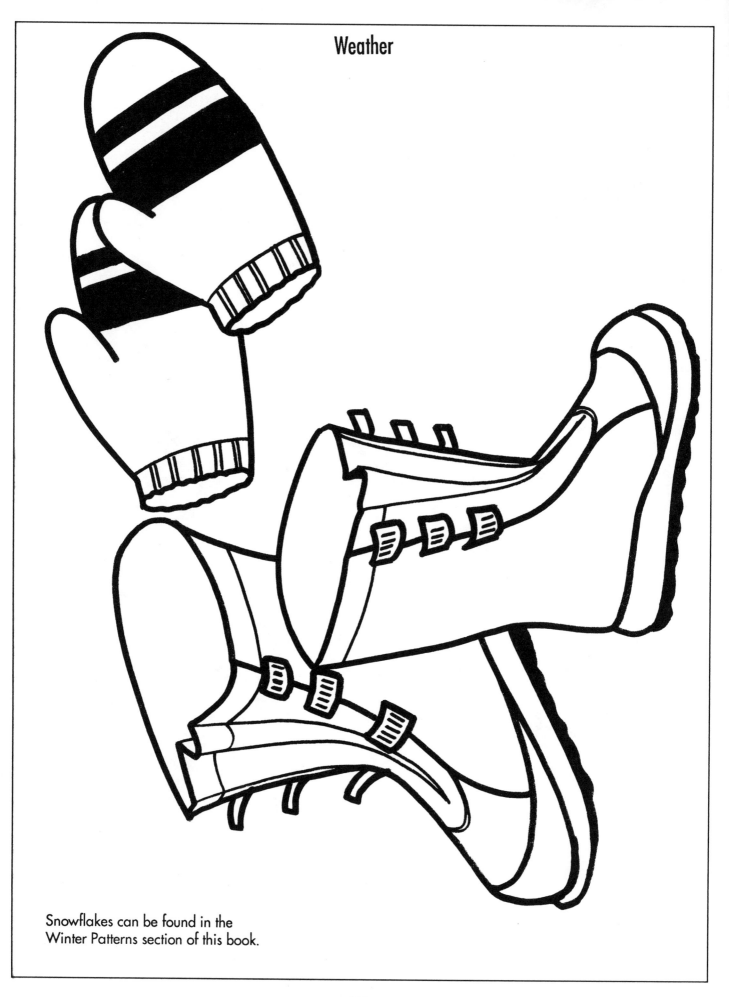

Snowflakes can be found in the
Winter Patterns section of this book.

GA1341

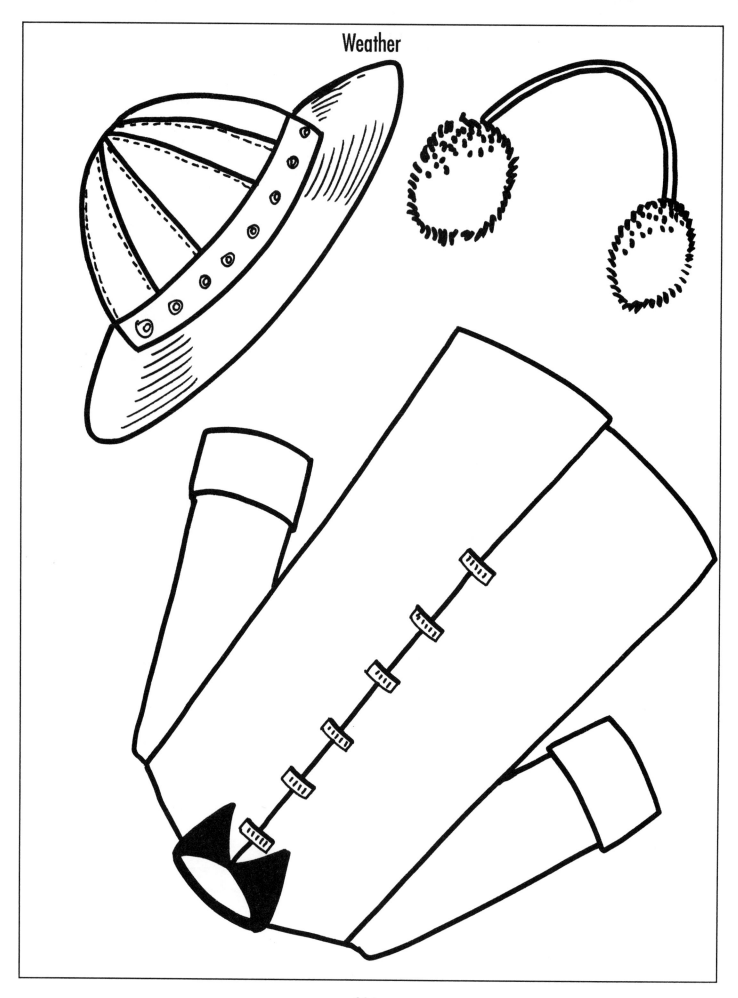

GA1341

GA1341

Food

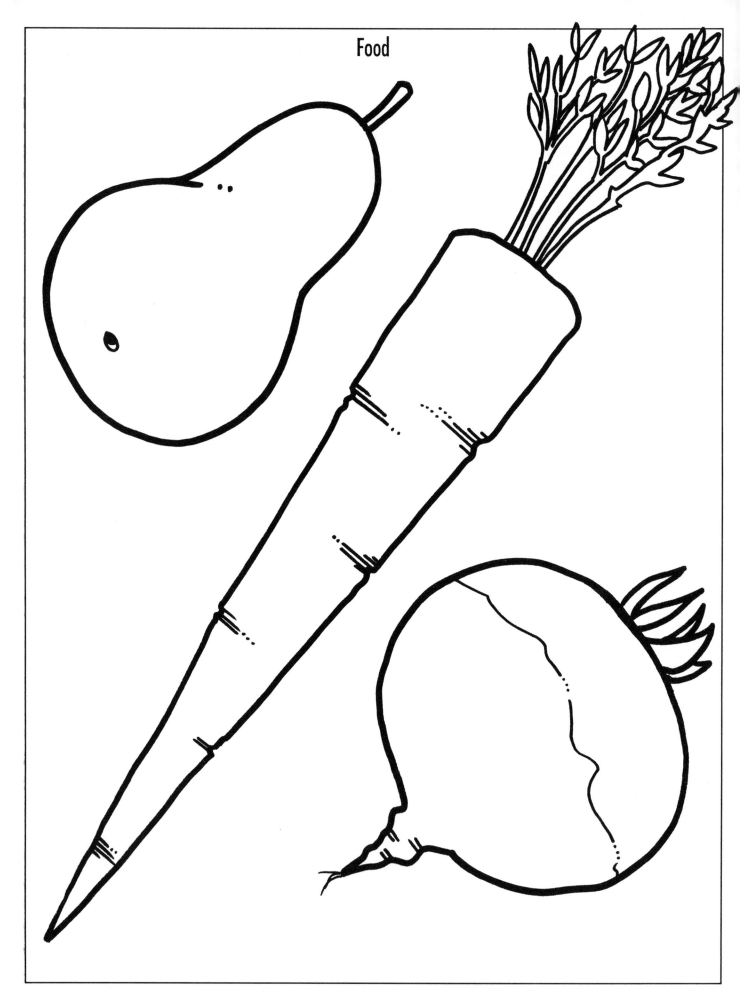

GA1341

GA1341

Food

308

GA1341

Food

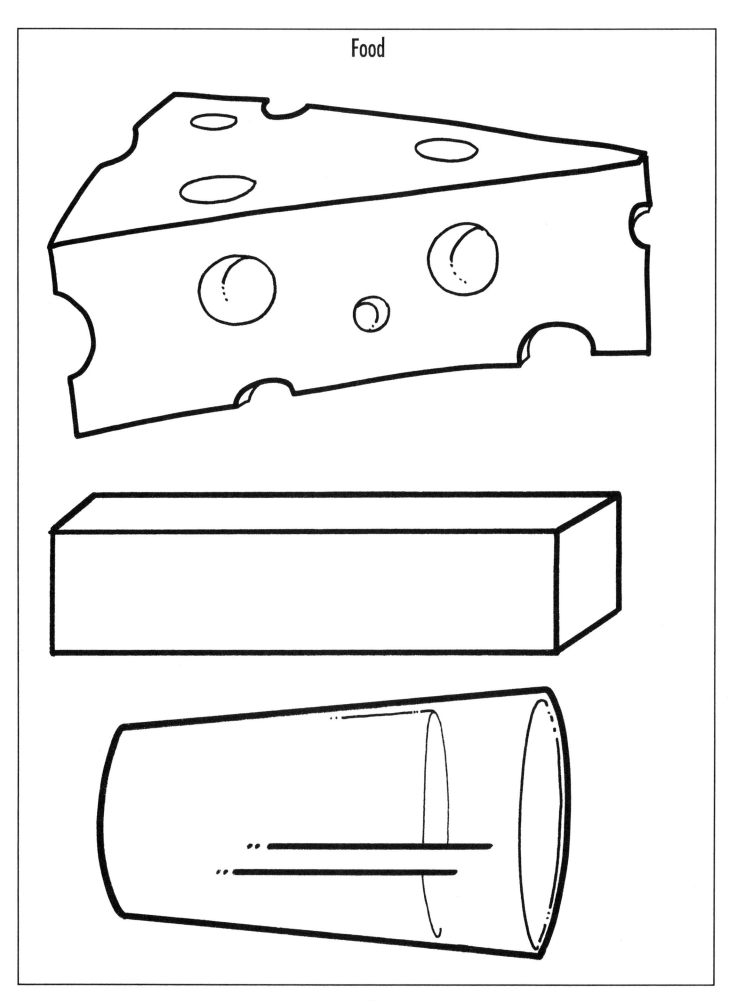

309

GA1341

Food

310

Food

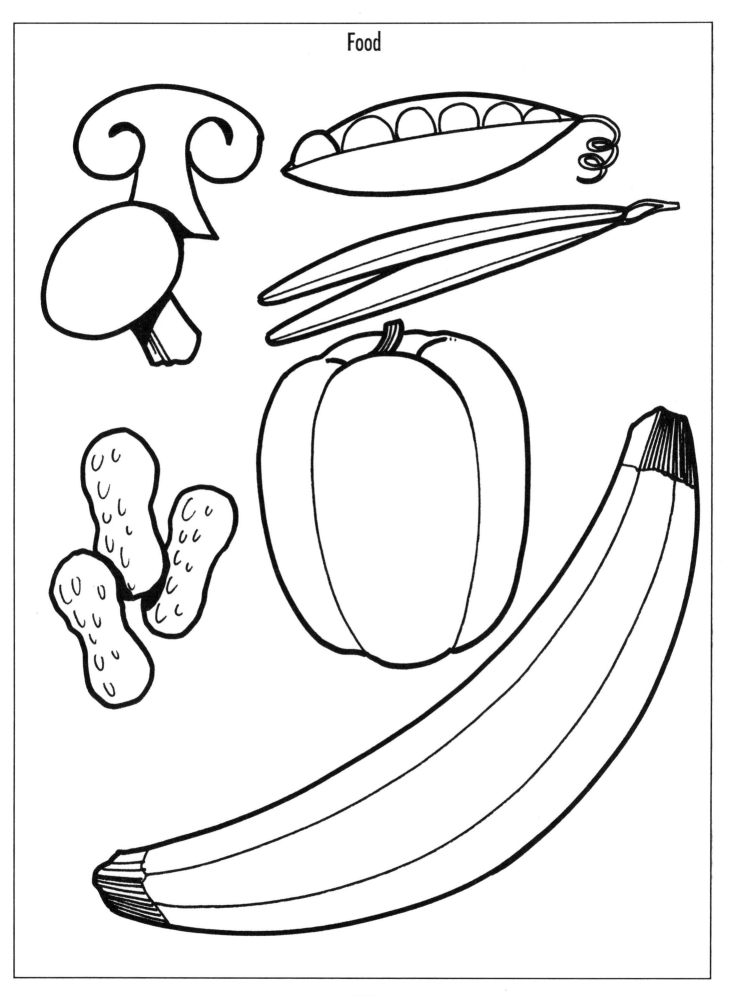

311

Food

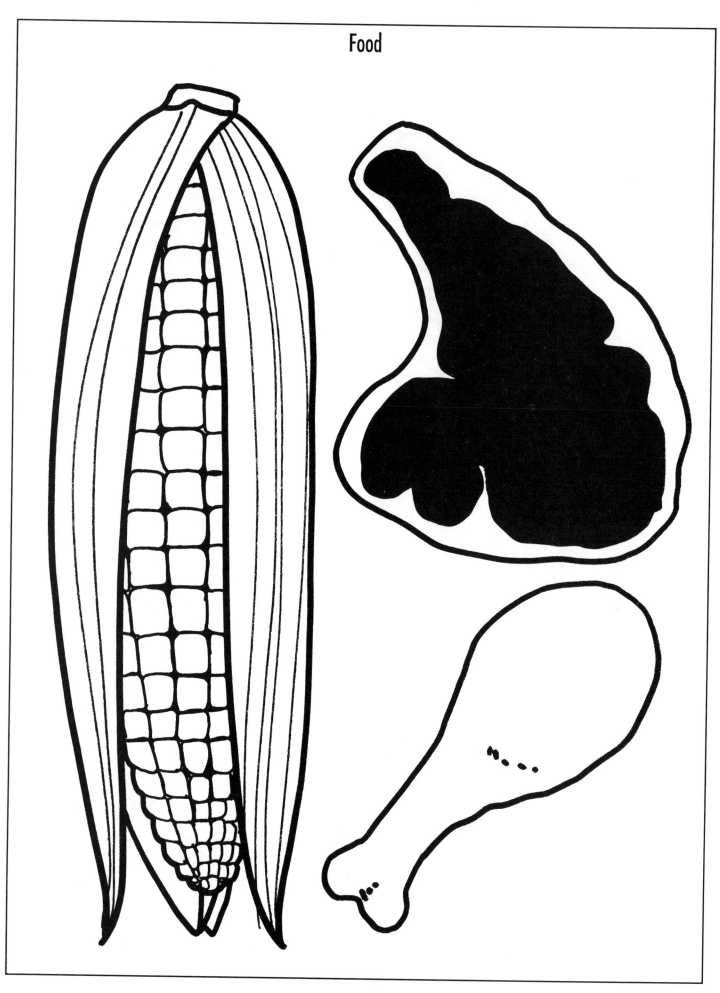

312

Food

313

314

Eastern Hemisphere

Western Hemisphere

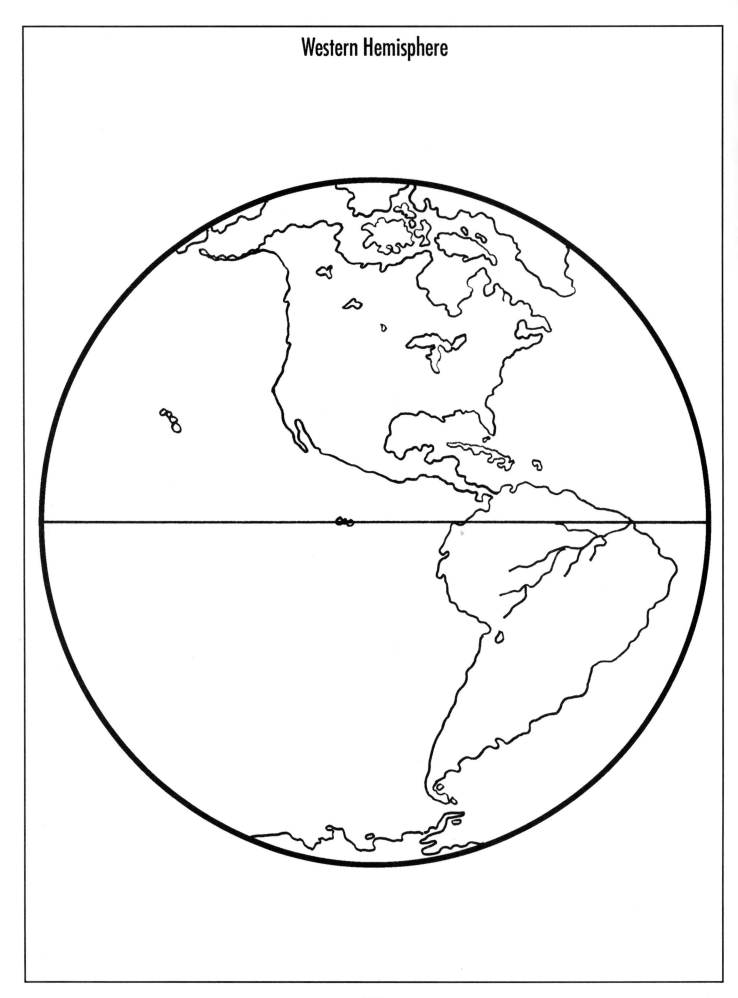

Inside the Earth

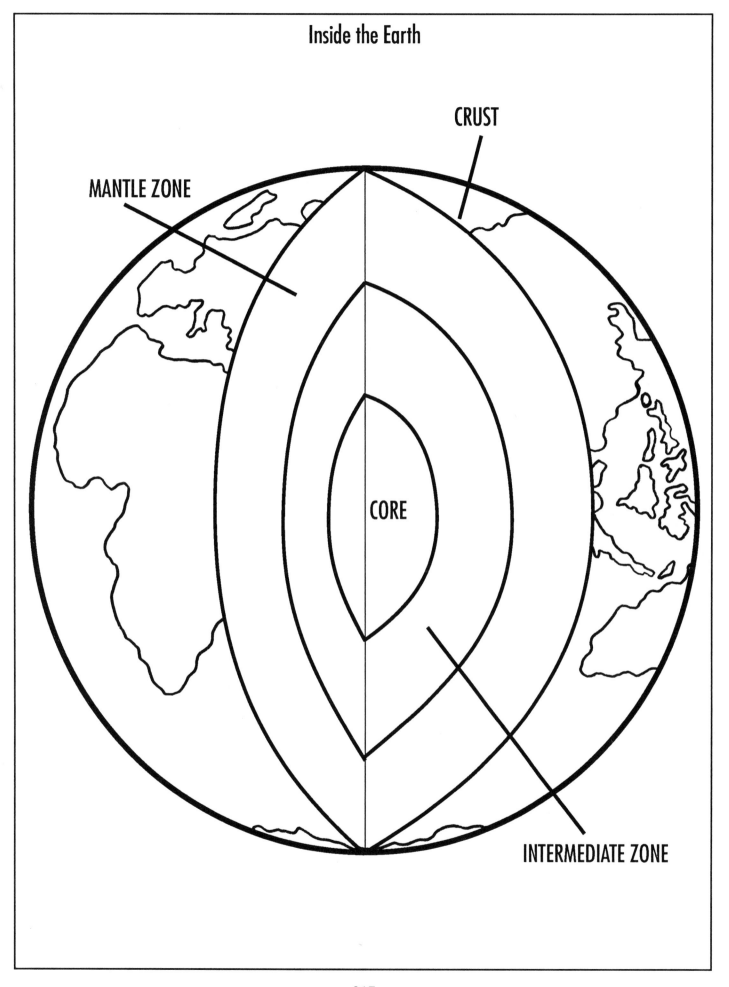

CRUST

MANTLE ZONE

CORE

INTERMEDIATE ZONE

GA1341

GA1341

GA1341

321

GA1341

Toys

324

GA1341

GA1341

GA1341

327

GA1341

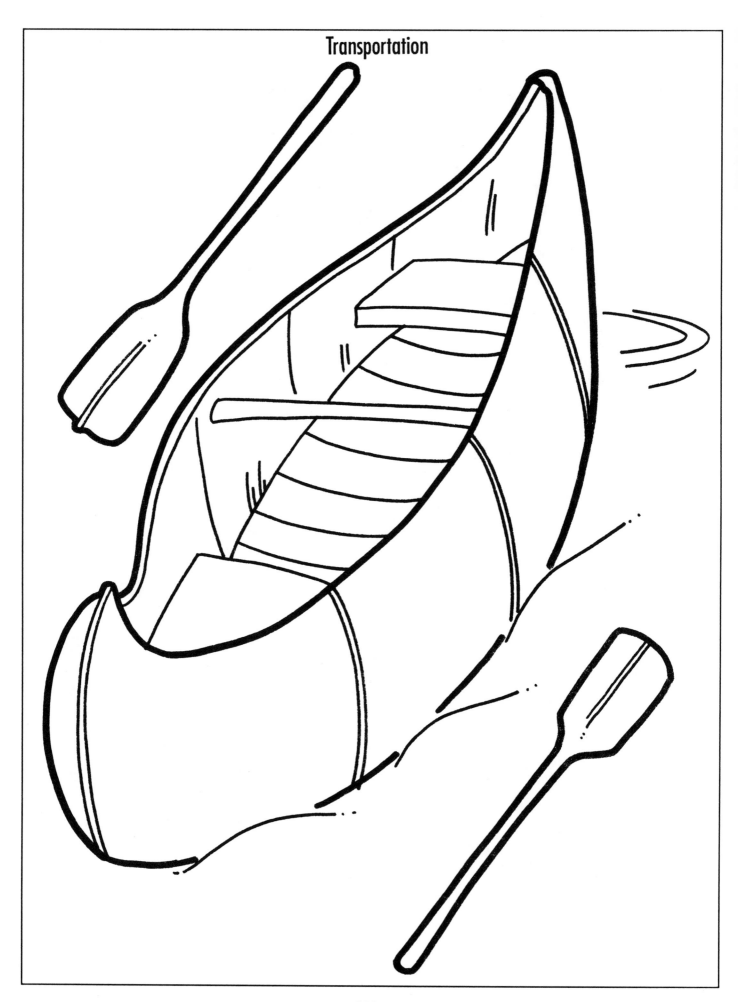

328

GA1341

Transportation

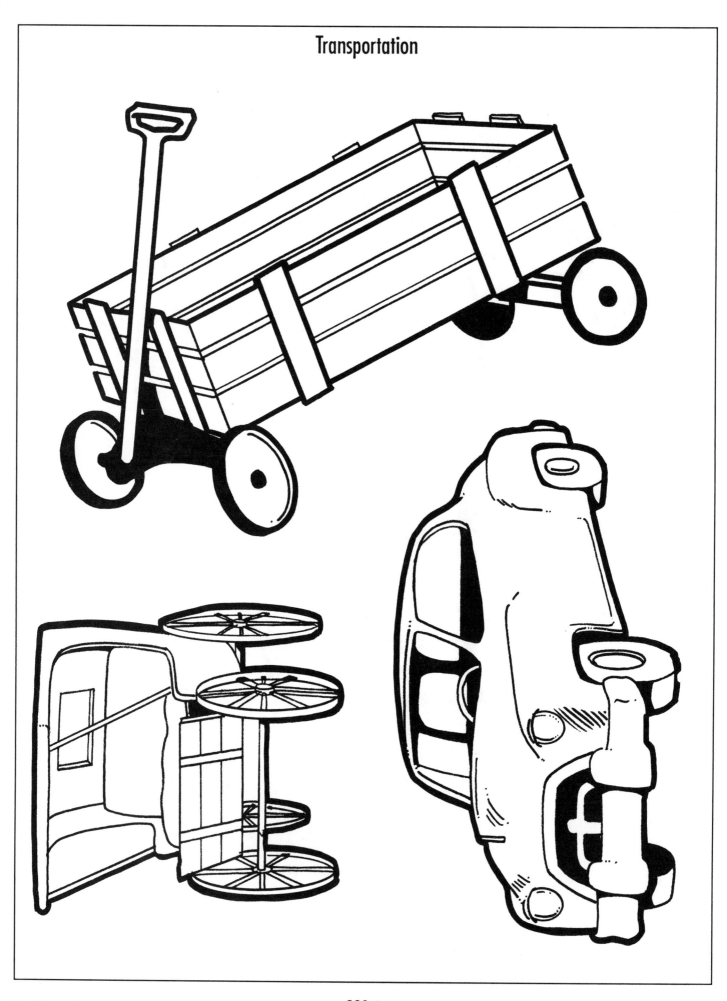

330

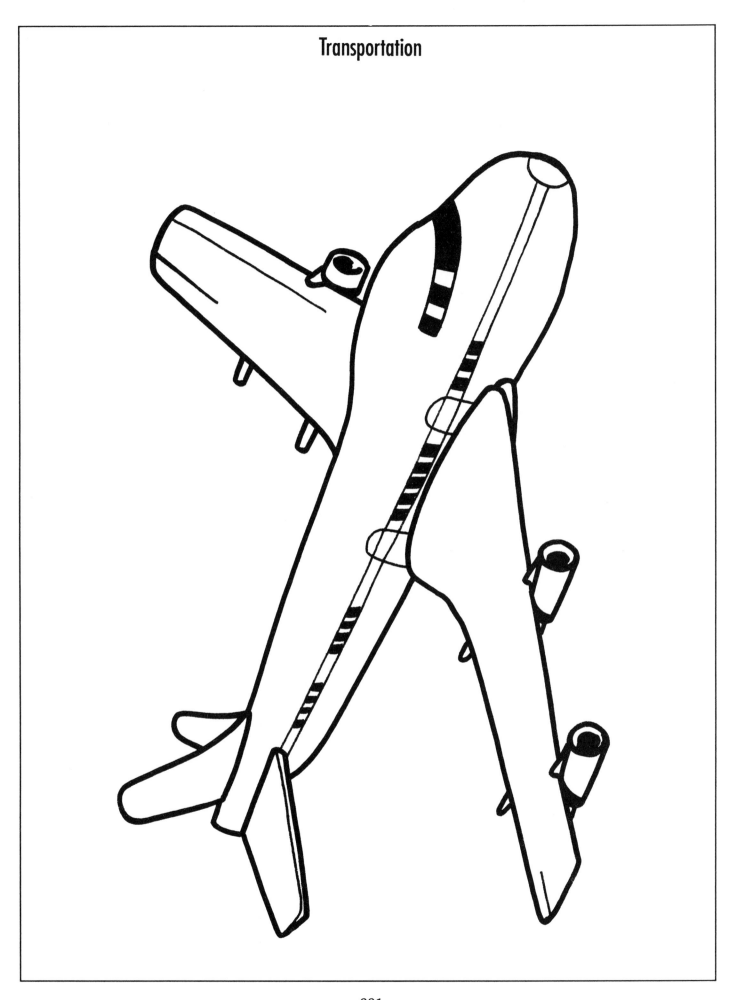

333

GA1341

U.S. MAIL

GA1341

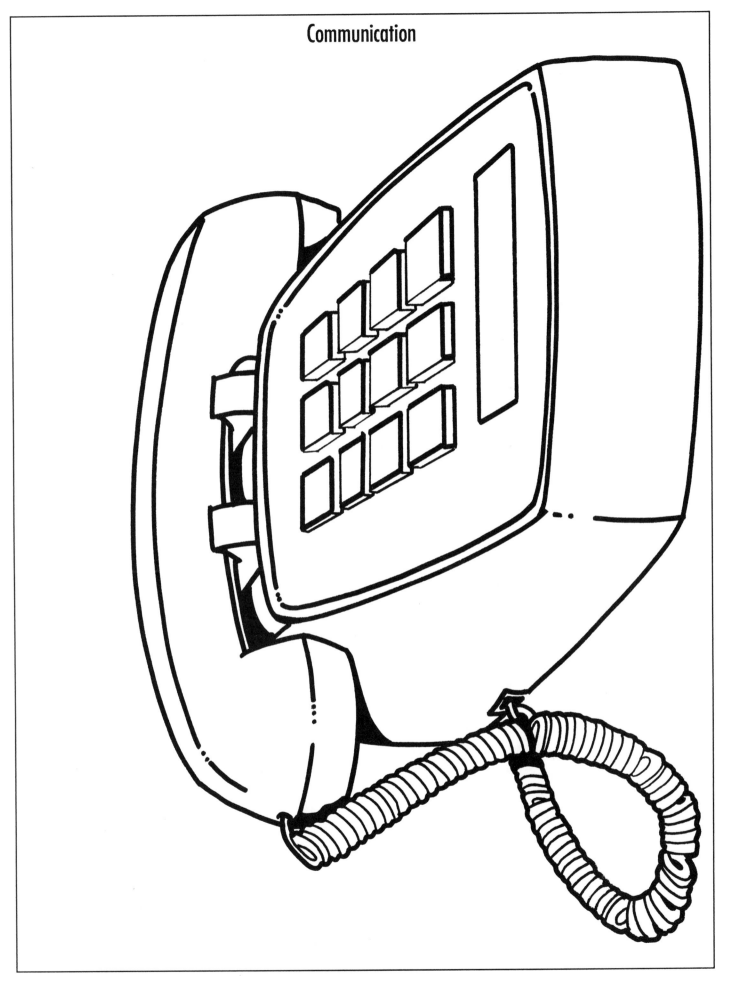

GA1341

336

Communication

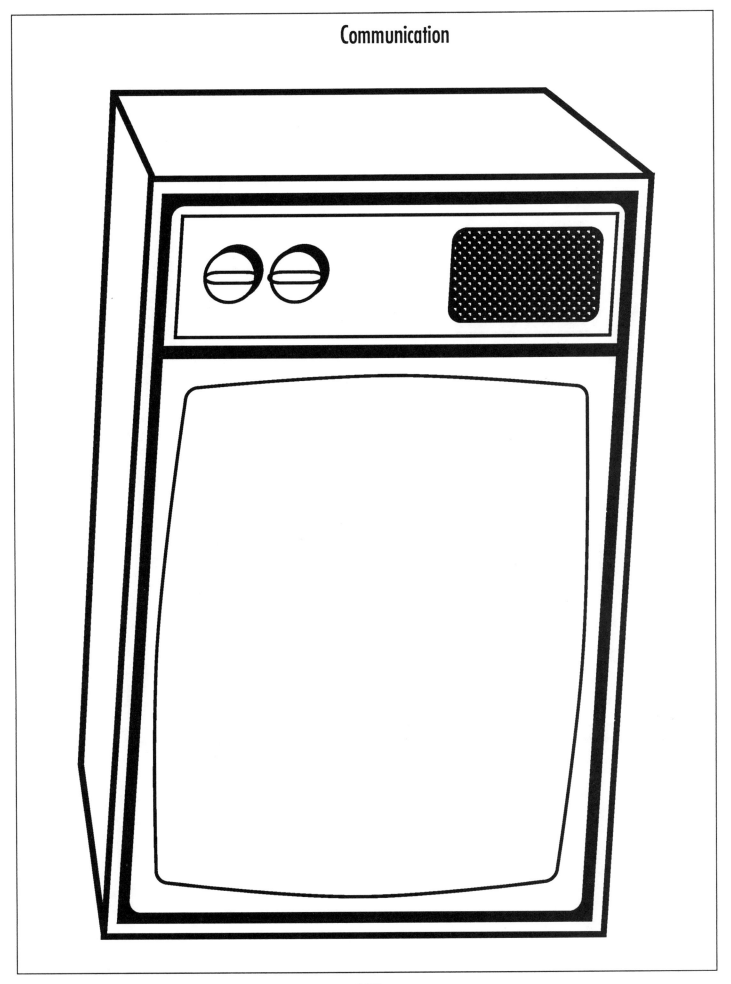

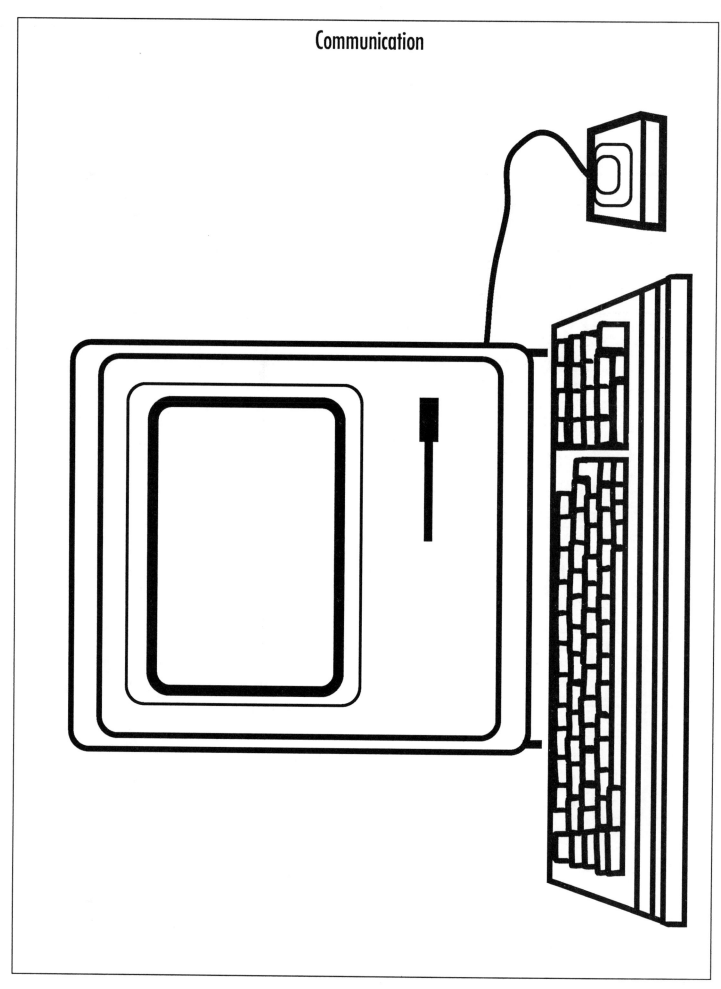

338

Birthday

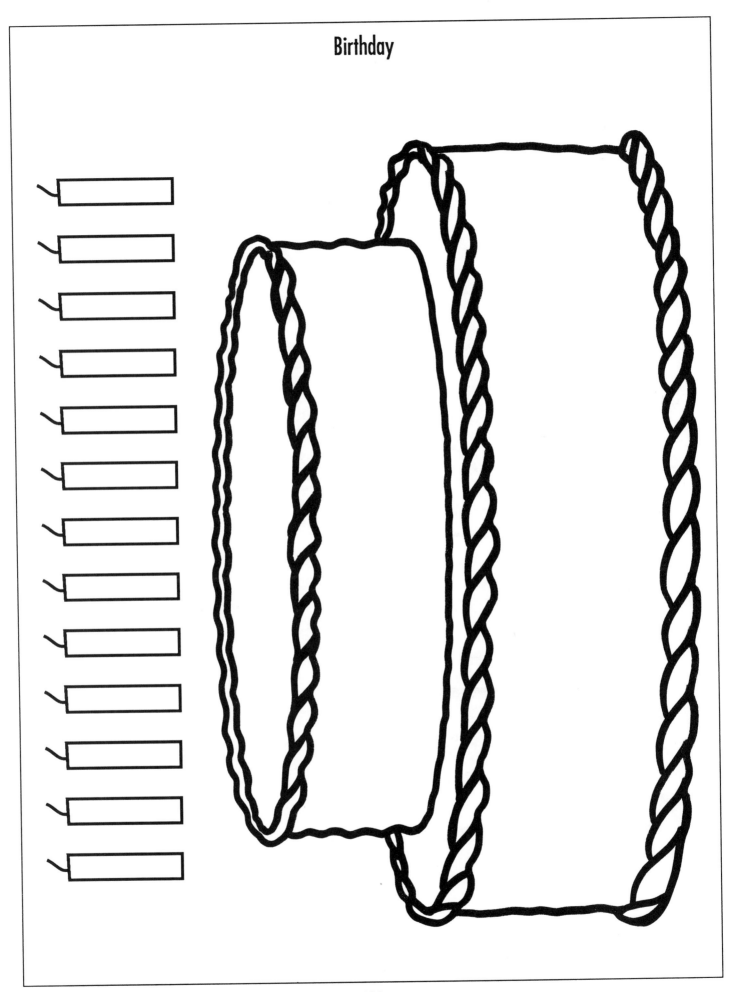

GA1341

340

Awards

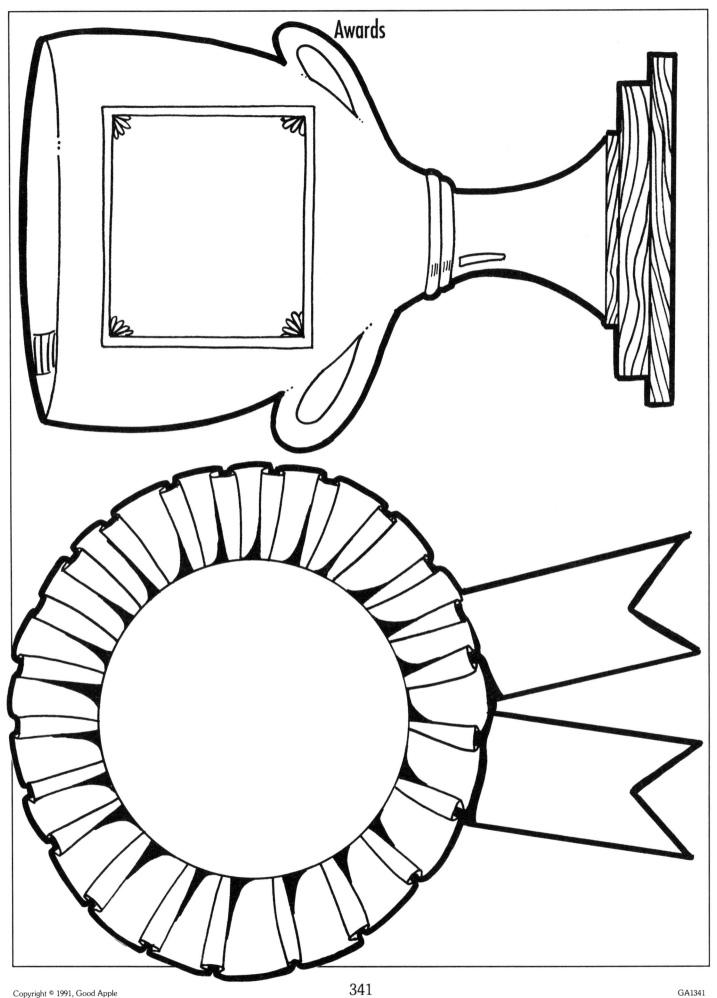

GA1341

BE A BIG CHEESE...
READ!!

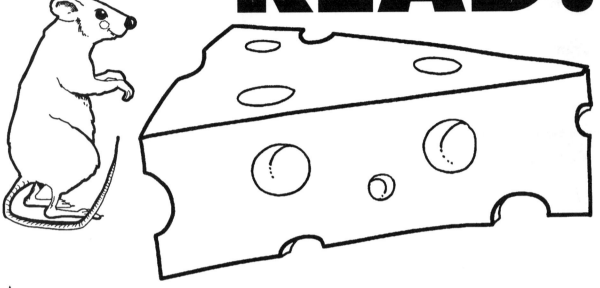

ALL-STAR
READERS

UP, UP AND AWAY!

GA1341

GA1341

WELCOME BACK!

BONUS BULLETIN BOARD IDEA

346

GA1341

HAPPY HALLOWEEN

CEMETERY

TRICK OR TREAT!

BONUS BULLETIN BOARD IDEA

GA1341

HERE'S TO YOUR GOOD HEALTH!!!

FAT SOURCES

COMPLEX CARBOHYDRATES

PROTEIN SOURCES

BONUS BULLETIN BOARD IDEA

GA1341